CHEYENNE WARRIOR

The Original Screenplay
with Author Commentary
by

Michael B. Druxman

Michael B. Druxman (signature)

The Center Press

Cheyenne Warrior:
The Original Screenplay
With Author Commentary
Preface and Afterward
Copyright ©1998 by Michael B. Druxman
Copyright Screenplay ©1994 The Pacific Trust

Acknowledgements

Grateful acknowledgement is made for permission to reprint photos from the following: Book cover photo art courtesy of Concorde/New Horizons Corp. who own the photo rights for **Cheyenne Warrior**; Photos from the movie **Cheyenne Warrior** courtesy of Concorde New Horizons Corp.; Other permission to reprint photos from the movie **Cheyenne Warrior** courtesy of Dan Haggarty, Bo Hopkins, Dan Clark, Pato Hoffmann, Patricia Van Ingen, and Rick Dean.

Special thanks to Ed Reilly for helping to make this book possible.

All rights Reserved.

No part of this book may by reproduced in any form, or by any electronic or mechanical means, including information storage or retrieval systems, without the written permission from the publisher, except by a reviewer who may quote brief passages in a review.

Library of Congress Cataloging-in-Publication Data

Druxman, Michael B., 1941-
    Cheyenne Warrior: the original screenplay with author commentary by Michael B. Druxman.
    p.   cm.
    ISBN 1-889198-03-X
    I. Cheyenne Warrior (Motion picture)   II. Title.
PN1997.C456   1998
791.43'72--dc21   97-46522
                                                                                    CIP

This is a work of fiction. Any resemblance to actual events or persons, living or dead, is entirely coincidental.

Published by
    The Center Press
    30961 W. Agoura Road Suite 223-B
    Westlake Village, CA 91361

Cover design photos courtesy of Concorde/New Horizons Corp.
Cover design: by Bart Design Associates
Book design: by Bart Design Associates
Printed in USA

10 9 8 7 6 5 4 3 2 1

For All Native Americans.

Through their innate dignity,
they are overcoming their
victimization in one of the most
shameful chapters of American history.

Other Books by

Michael B. Druxman

How to Write a Story...Any Story:
THE ART OF STORYTELLING

THE MUSICAL: From Broadway to Hollywood

ONE GOOD FILM DESERVES ANOTHER

CHARLTON HESTON

MERV

MAKE IT AGAIN, SAM

BASIL RATHBONE: His Life and His Films

PAUL MUNI: His Life and His Films

CONTENTS

Preface 3

The Original Screenplay 9

Afterword 161

Cast and Crew 175

PREFACE

Why **Cheyenne Warrior?**

<u>Cheyenne</u> <u>Warrior</u> had an *extremely* long gestation period. Somewhere around twenty years in length.

The basic idea for the story came to me in the early 1970s. I wanted to do **<u>The</u> <u>King</u> <u>and</u> <u>I</u>**...without music...as a western.

The "King," in this case, would be an Indian chief of some sort, and the "I" (or the "Anna" character) would be a white woman who "invades" his territory. Their relationship would evolve along the general plot lines of the classic Rodgers and Hammerstein musical.

Hollywood wasn't making many westerns back then, so I put my story on a mental back burner and turned my attention to other, more profitable, endeavors, such as books, a monthly magazine column, stage plays and, ultimately, screenplays.

Yet, being a western buff, I never completely forgot my story concept. I bided my time, waiting for the western cycle to come around again.

The **Lonesome Dove** mini-series (1989) and **Dances With Wolves** (1990) resurrected the western. I finally sat down and wrote my script, which I called *The* **Cheyenne Warrior**. It was completed and copyrighted in 1991.

Cheyenne Warrior was filmed during the late summer of 1993, opened the following August in a small Florida movie theater (to satisfy a Screen Actors Guild requirement), then was shuffled directly into the home video/laser disc and cable television marketplace.

To the best of my knowledge, this is the first time that the original screenplay of a motion picture that did not have a national theatrical release has ever been published in book form.

So, *why* **Cheyenne Warrior**?

The initial reviews on the movie were mixed. Certain critics praised the film; others faulted individual performances and, in some cases, aspects of the script. Frankly, I was happy with the way the final movie turned out. The producers and director made some cuts and minor changes to my original screenplay[*], yet, they'd remained essentially true to what I'd created and, I feel, that 95% of what is up on the screen is my writing.

Cheyenne Warrior sold well on video and laser disc, but when it started airing on HBO and The Movie Channel, a minor "phenomenon" began to happen.

Let me explain: There's a little game I play while browsing in video stores. A perplexed customer might ask me if a particular movie they're considering renting is "any good," and, if my answer is in the negative, I ask if they'd like me to suggest something.

Three guesses what movie I suggest.

---

[*] I strongly disagreed with them on one particular plot point.

I swear, the first time I did this, the customer replied "I've seen it two times. I love that movie."

"Thank you," I said, then revealed my connection to the film.

Hey, what's wrong with taking a bow?

And, that's not the only time this has happened. It's happened to me many times.

True, there've been more occasions when the person never heard of **Cheyenne Warrior**, or, after I'd suggested it, decided that they didn't want to rent it.** But what I gleaned from the positive experiences was the fact that people — women, in particular — who had seen the film liked it.

Indeed, it had "moved" them.

Some fan mail started arriving...all from women. The writers loved the movie. One woman from the East coast phoned me. "Why don't you write a sequel?" she asked. "We want to know what happens to Rebecca and Hawk."

Near the end of 1996, I attended a party where I met a Native American woman. During the course of the conversation, she remarked, "That's such a wonderful movie. It does so much to dignify and further the Native American cause."

"Gee," I said, taken aback. "I'm no crusader. I was just trying to spin a good yarn."

That conversation fired me. I began to surf the Internet, seeking references to my film.

That search led to two positive results. First, I met another Native American woman (via e-mail), an apparent activist, who lives in Michigan. She strongly echoed the sentiments of the first lady I'd encountered at the party.

** In those instances, I'd smile and do something nasty, like recommend the latest Steven Seagal movie.

Second, I came across a review of **Cheyenne Warrior**, located on the "**TV Guide** Entertainment Network," which blew me away. You'll forgive me if I quote it, in part:

"Combining an unusual appreciation of the vicissitudes of frontier life with an elegiac sense of the plight of native Americans, **Cheyenne Warrior** is a thinking man's western. It's a welcome throwback to the traditions of the genre, set against a breathtaking wilderness backdrop which virtually emerges as a character in itself....Overblown western dramas like **Wyatt Earp** and **Legends of the Fall** could have picked up a few lessons from this modest success."

About this same time, I had occasion to speak with Pato Hoffmann, who plays Hawk in the movie. He told me that he'd received a tremendous amount of fan mail praising **Cheyenne Warrior**...*from all over the world.*

I mentioned all of this to Sue Artof, owner of The Center Press, which was then in the process of publishing my book, **How to Write a Story...Any Story: THE ART OF STORYTELLING**. Intrigued, she investigated the niche market... several niches, actually...to see if there was any interest in a printed version of **Cheyenne Warrior**. She discovered that there was.

Certainly the book belonged on the store shelves next to other published screenplays, but, more importantly, the distributors felt that this particular work would appeal to readers of Western Americana, especially those interested in the Native American experience.

From my standpoint, I'm delighted to have my original story and screenplay presented to the public for the first time. Had this version been shot in its entirety, the finished film would have played closer to 2-hours, rather than its crisp 86-minute running time. Perhaps that would've been a mistake. Longer, after all, is not always better.

Here, however, both in the script and in its Afterword, people who've come to embrace the love story of Rebecca and Hawk can garner a more in-depth understanding of these characters, the tenuous time in which they lived and, finally, how their saga was brought to the screen.

CHEYENNE WARRIOR

The Original Screenplay

EXT. THE PRAIRIE. DAY.

CAMERA SWEEPS ACROSS a rolling grassland, stretching as far as the eye can see; comes to rest on a large herd of buffalo grazing peacefully.

The pastoral scene is interrupted suddenly by an O.S. SHOT. A large bull is struck in the head; collapses onto the ground.

The rest of the herd stirs uneasily, but does not move. Another O.S. SHOT, and a second animal is hit.

The herd panics; starts to run. More O.S. SHOTS. Two more buffalo hit the ground. The frightened animals continue to run.

CUT TO:

EXT. ANOTHER PART OF THE PRAIRIE. DAY.

Awhile later. UNDER THE CREDITS, three Cheyenne braves on horseback gallop over a hill. They are dressed in shirts and leggings made from buffalo hide, and have a string of six Indian ponies with them. They are armed with bow and arrow; front loading muskets. CAMERA TRACKS.

Heading the group is SOARS LIKE A HAWK, 28, a handsome warrior with strong, classic features. He rides a pinto. His feathers and other adornments mark him as a gallant warrior chief who has distinguished himself in battle on many occasions. Indeed, Hawk is a charismatic, level-headed, leader, in line to become a Council chief.

Riding just behind Hawk is SPOTTED FACE, 25, his cousin. Also a dauntless fighter, Spotted Face is a sullen man. He gets his name from multiple scars he received from a fall he took onto some rocks many years ago.

The third brave leads the string of ponies. He is LITTLE RABBIT, 25, a short, quiet man, known for his speed at foot racing.

The Indians continue riding across the plain, then as CREDITS END, they reach the top of a small rise; quickly rein their horses. Shocked, troubled expressions cross their faces, as they see:

A few hundred yards away are the carcasses of a half dozen slain buffalo; their hides taken. Scavenger birds pick at the abundance of meat that has been left to rot.

The Indians react with anger. Spotted Face mutters curses in Cheyenne. Hawk remains silent, but his inner rage is tinged with a look of melancholy.

Little Rabbit points off to the right of the carcasses.

Relatively fresh wagon tracks trail off into the distance.

The Indians begin to follow the tracks.

CUT TO:

EXT. STILL ANOTHER PART OF THE PRAIRIE. DAY.

The tracks are being made by a battered, horse-drawn, open wagon, proceeding along the plain. A pile of buffalo skins are in the back of the conveyance, which has two men riding in silence on the front seat. The driver is DANIEL KEARNEY, 30, a stocky, red bearded Irishman with broken teeth, a broken nose, and who speaks with an accent that betrays his origins. Sometimes he can play the charming rogue, but on most occasions Kearney's innate malicious self is apparent. Over clothing that is about as filthy as he, Kearney wears an extra large coat made from buffalo hide, and an old wide-brimmed hat. A Spencer repeating rifle is at his side.

His companion is OTTO NIELSEN, 23, average height; considerably less experienced in the ways of the world than Kearney. His features are essentially boyish, his beard is sparse, but he, too, possesses a broken nose and is in need of a bath. He wears a cloth coat; a wool cap. He amuses himself by picking his nose, as he grips a Sharps breech-loading rifle. Both men also have Colt revolvers stuck into their belts.

The wagon reaches a jagged bluff, overlooking a narrow river. Downstream and up from the other side of the river bank is a primitive trading post, a windowless log structure with a wood roof and porch. A sign atop the roof reads: "Barkley's." There is a privy out back, a lean-to and a corral confining four horses. An empty open wagon is parked behind the corral. Stacked next to the main building is a large stockpile of cut firewood. Nearby is a covered prairie schooner, drawn by two oxen.

Kearney maneuvers his wagon toward a tenuous road cut into the bluff, which leads down to the river bank.

Far in the distance loom the Rocky Mountains.

CUT TO:

EXT. TRADING POST YARD. DAY.

CYRUS BARKLEY, 58, owner of the trading post, is squatting, as he examines the swollen front leg of one of the schooner's oxen. He's a crusty, beefy gent with a scruffy beard, missing several front teeth, and a knife scar across his cheek. He walks with a limp; wears buckskins.

Standing next to him is MATTHEW CARVER, 22, a very tall, husky, unworldly young man, attired in a jacket and worn work clothing suitable for travel.

His pretty, willowy blond wife, REBECCA CARVER, 20, sits on the front seat of the wagon, listening to the men converse. She wears a cotton dress, somewhat soiled from weeks on the prairie. A buffalo robe is around her shoulders. Rebecca is small, a seemingly shy girl, often hesitant to speak her mind. She is five months pregnant. A Henry rifle leans against the seat next to her.

Barkley stands, spits a wad of tobacco onto the ground, as he indicates the ox.

>   BARKLEY
>   (To Matthew)
>   It ain't broke... but this here
>   animal ain't goin' to get you
>   to Oregon, sonny.... Won't get
>   you half way up the mountain.

>   MATTHEW
>   (Mutters)
>   Shit!

Tears of frustration well up in Rebecca's eyes, but she remains silent.

>   BARKLEY
>   Hell, by the time that leg heals,
>   there'll be snow in the pass.
>   (Heads back toward
>   the building)
>   You're gonna be stuck here
>   'til Spring.

>   REBECCA
>   Matt, what're we gonna do?

>   MATTHEW
>   (Calls after Barkley)
>   Ain't there another way round?

                    BARKLEY
                (Without stopping)
        Nope.
He enters the trading post. Matt glances up at his wife; avoids eye contact.

                    REBECCA
        Matt?

He scowls at her; follows Barkley toward the trading post. Behind him, across the river, we SEE Kearney and Nielsen's wagon reaching the bottom of the bluff.

                                            CUT TO:

INT. TRADING POST. DAY.

A large shabby, dark room, well stocked on one side with food staples and other goods (i.e. blankets, colorful clothing, muskets, ammunition, metal knives, kettles and hatchets, trinkets, etc.) for trading with the Indians and white settlers, and on the other with buffalo hides and beaver pelts for shipment back East. In the rear is a back door, braced shut with a two-by-four, and Barkley's living quarters, consisting of a tacky bed, wood rocking chair, small table and a metal stove.

Barkley enters; crosses to behind the dusty counter and starts checking merchandise. Matthew stands in the doorway.

                    MATTHEW
            Ain't there someplace 'round
            here I can buy another ox?

                    BARKLEY
                (Shakes head)
            Damn fool! Should've waited....
            Come west with a wagon train.

                    MATTHEW
        Couldn't wait.
                    BARKLEY
              (Beat; matter-of-fact)
        Everybody's runnin' away from
        somethin', sonny.... What's yours?
        The conscription?

Matthew hesitates; nods.

                    BARKLEY
              (Continuing)
        Seems like half the folk headin' west these
        days are tryin' to avoid that ruckus.
              (Chuckles)
        Can't blame you. From what I hear
        tell, those Southern boys are beatin'
        the crap outta you Blue Bellies.

                    MATTHEW
        I got kin in Virginia. I ain't
        goin' to start shootin' at 'em.

                    BARKLEY
              (Beat)
        Sure you ain't just plain yellow?

                    MATTHEW
        I ain't yellow!

                    BARKLEY
        Good. Cause, if you are, you sure as
        hell ain't gonna make it out here.
              (Tosses him a hunk of tobacco)
        Have a chaw.

Matthew catches the tobacco; looks at it without much enthusiasm.

EXT. TRADING POST YARD. DAY.

Rebecca sits in the schooner, shivering under the buffalo robe, as she remains lost within her worries.

Kearney and Nielsen's wagon draws up beside the schooner. Kearney spots Rebecca; beams a suggestive grin in her direction.

                    KEARNEY
                (To Nielsen)
            Now, ain't she a beauty?

                    NIELSEN
                (Nods; lecherous)
            Sure's pretty.

Rebecca blanches; scoots along the seat away from them.

                    KEARNEY
                (Tips hat)
            Daniel Kearney from County Donegal.
                (Indicating Nielsen)
            My mate, Mr. Nielsen.

Nielsen grins. Rebecca doesn't.

                    KEARNEY
                (Continuing)
            Would you be headin' west, ma'm?

                    REBECCA
                (Nods; indicates building)
            My... my husband's inside.

                        KEARNEY
          No offense, ma'm.... I was admirin'
          that new Henry.
                    (Indicates rifle next to her)
          I hear it's quite a rifle.
                    (Jumps down from his seat)
          Would you mind if I take a look at it?

He reaches out for the rifle, but Rebecca grabs it; points it at him.

                        KEARNEY
          Ma'm... I mean you no harm.

                        MATTHEW (O.S.)
          What do you want, mister?

Matthew steps off the porch of the trading post; walks over toward the wagons. Barkley watches from the porch.

                        KEARNEY
                    (To Matthew; sizing him up)
          Ah! You must be the strapping
          young bridegroom.

His hand brushes the Colt revolver stuck into his belt.

                        MATTHEW
                    (Fist clenched)
          I asked you what you wanted.

                        KEARNEY
                    (Impressed with
                    Matthew's size)
          Well, I wasn't wantin' to fight ya.
          I'll tell you that.... I was just bein'
          sociable. Tryin' to strike up a
          conversation with yer missus.

The men study each other.

                    MATTHEW
            He bother you, Becky?

                    REBECCA
              (Shakes head; slightly
               embarrassed)
            He wanted to look at the rifle.

                    MATTHEW
            Don't you got yer own rifle, mister?

                    KEARNEY
              (Chuckles; points to
               his wagon)
            Just a Spencer.
              (To Nielsen)
            Show 'im, Otto.

Nielsen tosses the Spencer down to Matthew. He keeps his Sharps handy on his lap. Matthew holds the Spencer, never taking his eyes off of Kearney.

                    MATTHEW
              (Indicating the Henry)
            Let 'im see it, Becky.

Rebecca, reluctantly, hands the Henry down to Kearney. The men examine each other's weapon... while really sizing up the other.

                    KEARNEY
              (Aiming into the
               distance)
            Fine weapon. You wouldn't be
            wantin' to be sell it, would ya?

                    MATTHEW
            Not hardly. Was a gift from my pa.

Kearney's grip tightens on the Henry. Matthew continues to stare him down. Nielsen waits for a sign from his partner.

A tense moment, then out of the corner of his eye, Kearney spots Barkley watching from the porch.

>KEARNEY
>(Beat)
>Well, then... it would be a sin to
>sell it, wouldn't it now?

He hands the Henry back to Matthew, who returns the Spencer to him.

On the porch, Barkley emits a low whistle of relief.

>BARKLEY
>(To himself)
>The boy's not yellow.

Kearney tips his hat to Matthew and Rebecca; indicates Barkley.

>KEARNEY
>If you'll be excusin' me, I've got some
>business to transact with the trader there.

He strolls over toward Barkley. Nielsen jumps down from the wagon. He gives Rebecca one last lewd glance, then follows Kearney over to the porch.

>BARKLEY
>What can I do fer you gents?

>KEARNEY
>Got some buffalo hides to trade.

>BARKLEY
>That's what I'm here for.

Kearney and Nielsen follow him into the building.

Matthew moves over to Rebecca.

>   MATTHEW
>   (With some concern)
>   You feel all right, Becky?

>   REBECCA
>   I guess so.
>   (Hesitates, then
>   blurts out)
>   But, Matt... what are we gonna do?

>   MATTHEW
>   (Snaps)
>   Becky, if I knew what we were gonna
>   do, we'd damn well do it!

Again, Rebecca's eyes become slightly moist.

>   MATTHEW
>   (Beat; gentler)
>   Mr. Barkley asked us to stay
>   for supper.

                                             CUT TO:

EXT. TRADING POST YARD. DUSK.

Kearney and Nielsen, their wagon filled with supplies, head out onto the prairie, away from the river.

Barkley, Matthew and Rebecca stand on the porch, watching them depart.

                    BARKLEY
          Don't like them fellas. Their
          daddies should've done folks a
          favor an' hung 'em when they was
          born.

The trio enter the building.

                                        CUT TO:

EXT. THE PRAIRIE. DUSK

As the wagon heads away from the trading post, Kearney turns to Nielsen.

                    KEARNEY
          Otto, me boy, I sure liked the
          feel of that Henry.

                    NIELSEN
               (Giggles)
          I sure liked the look of that woman.

                    KEARNEY
               (Beams)
          That, too.

The wagon continues to move off into the distance.

                                        CUT TO:

INT. TRADING POST. NIGHT.

The room is lit by two oil lamps. Barkley, Matthew and Rebecca sit around a table near the back of the room. They are eating their meal... a kind of prairie stew. The older man quickly devours what's on his plate. Matthew and Rebecca are more tentative.

                    BARKLEY
               (Amused)
          Don't fret none, ma'm. First time
          they told me what was in this prairie
          stew, I near turned green myself....
          But, ya know, you get to like it....
          Rattlesnake... prairie dog.... They're
          good eatin'. "Delicacies," they'd call
          'em back East.

                    REBECCA
               (Forcing a smile)
     It's... different.

She brushes a section of the thin carpet of dust off the table; stares at her plate.

                                        CUT TO:

EXT. THE RIVER. NIGHT.

The moon is full, as Hawk, Spotted Face and Little Rabbit, with the string of ponies, make their way down the side of the bluff.

                                        CUT TO:

INT. TRADING POST. NIGHT.

Matthew and Barkley are at the table, drinking coffee. Rebecca, having taken charge of the kitchen, moves about with a large coffee pot, refilling the men's cups.

BARKLEY
(Musing)
No, I came out from the Ohio near twenty years ago.... Made friends with the Cheyenne. Married me the chief's sister so's I'd stay friends with 'em.

REBECCA
(Taken aback)
You.... You married an Indian!?!

BARKLEY
(Nods)
Damn good woman she was, too. I'm a lazy sort, so it was kinda handy to have her around to do the heavy work.

MATTHEW
She died?

BARKLEY
(Nods)
Last year of the fever.... Kinda miss 'er. 'Cept fer her gabberin'.... Ya know, there's nothin' worse'n' havin' a woman nag at ya in Cheyenne.

MATTHEW
Oh, I don't know....

Rebecca gives him a nasty look.

CUT TO:

EXT. THE RIVER. NIGHT.

Hawk and his companions cross the river.

INT. TRADING POST. NIGHT.

Barkley, Matthew and Rebecca are as we last saw them.

          BARKLEY
The Cheyenne are a right honorable
people. Great traders. Trade me
the same horses over an' over again.
    (Beat)
It's the damn Pawnee you gotta be
careful of. They'll shake hands with
ya with their right hand, an' cut off
yer balls with their left.

          REBECCA
    (Shocked)
My goodness!

          BARKLEY
    (Chagrined)
Excuse me, m'am. Been away from
white society too long.... But,
don't you worry none.... The Pawnee
live down south a ways. Don't see much
of 'em 'round here.

Outside, the SOUND of horses. Barkley snaps alert.

EXT. TRADING POST YARD. NIGHT.

Hawk and his companions rein their horses outside the building.

INT. TRADING POST. NIGHT.

Barkley, Matthew and Rebecca are as we last saw them.

BARKLEY
Appears like we got company.

He gets up from the table. Grabs a Sharps rifle leaning against the wall. Rebecca is alarmed, as is Matthew, who is without his Henry.

BARKLEY
(Continuing; to Matthew)
Where's yer rifle, boy?

MATTHEW
I.... I left it in the wagon.

BARKLEY
(Frustrated sigh)
Didn't yer pa ever tell ya that you never go any place....
(Beat)
Ferget it!

He grabs a Colt revolver from a holster that hangs on the wall; tosses it to Matthew.

BARKLEY
(Mutters; to himself)
They breed 'em dumber and dumber every year.

Barkley carries an oil lamp, as the two men move toward the front door.

BARKLEY
(Continuing; over his shoulder to Rebecca)
Ma'm, you best duck down behind the counter 'til we know who's out here.

Rebecca moves to behind the counter.

                    BARKLEY
               (Continuing; to
                Matthew)
          Don't shoot nuthin'... 'less I
          shoot first. You understand?

                    MATTHEW
          Yes, sir.

Barkley opens the door; steps out. Matthew remains inside the door.

EXT. TRADING POST YARD. NIGHT.

Holding the lamp in one hand and his Sharps in the other, Barkley steps out onto the porch; peers into the darkness.

                    BARKLEY
          Who's out there?

Hawk, on horseback, emerges from the shadows, holding the Henry. His two companions, also mounted, move up to either side of him. Spotted Face holds Rebecca's buffalo robe. They remain several yards from the building, silhouetted in the moonlight.

                    BARKLEY
               (Continuing)
          Hawk?

Hawk's reaction is well-mannered; reserved. His companions remain poker-faced.

                    HAWK
          Barkley.

Hawk nods to the trader, who beams a smile.

                    BARKLEY
               (Sincere)
          Good to see ya, Hawk.
               (Noticing the string
               of ponies)
          You come to trade?

INT. TRADING POST. NIGHT.

Matthew and Rebecca listen apprehensively to the conversation outside.

EXT. TRADING POST YARD. NIGHT.

Barkley and the Indians are as we last saw them.

                    HAWK
               (Nods; matter-of-fact)
          We trade.

                    BARKLEY
               (Friendly)
          Come on inside. Have some supper.

                    HAWK
               (Gestures with the
               Henry)
          Whites inside?

                    BARKLEY
          Yeah. Come meet 'em. They're nice folks.

                    HAWK
               (Beat)
          I meet them.

Hawk slides off his horse, and carrying the Henry, walks toward the building. As he mounts the stairs, Barkley glances over toward Spotted Face and Little Rabbit.

> BARKLEY
> (Gestures to come)
> You ain't hungry?

Spotted Face and Little Rabbit dismount; follow Hawk up onto the porch. Spotted Face brings the buffalo robe. Both men carry their muskets.

INT. TRADING POST. NIGHT.

A jittery Matthew and Rebecca back away from the door, as Barkley enters, followed by Hawk. Matthew keeps the Colt pressed to the side of his leg. Rebecca stays in shadow, so that her features are not well defined. Spotted Face and Little Rabbit remain in the open doorway.

> BARKLEY
> Folks, I want you to meet
> Soars Like a Hawk. Call 'im
> Hawk fer short. He's a Cheyenne
> warrior. Could be chief one day.
> (Indicates Hawk's companions)
> An' that's Spotted Face and Little
> Rabbit. Don't take much brains
> to figure out which is which.
> (To Hawk)
> This here's Mr. an' Mrs. Carver...
> from the land east of the Ohio.

Hawk and the Carvers study each other for a moment.

> HAWK
> (Gestures toward outside
> with Henry)
> Your wagon?

                    REBECCA
              (Surprised, whispers
               to Matthew)
         He speaks English!

                    BARKLEY
         'Course he speaks English. It
         were a lot easier teachin' him
         than me learnin' Cheyenne.

                    MATTHEW
              (To Hawk, indicating
               rifle)
         That's my Henry.

                    HAWK
         Your rifle?

                    MATTHEW
         Yeah.

His grip tightens on the Colt, but he doesn't raise it.

Spotted Face tosses the buffalo robe onto the floor in front of him.

                    HAWK
         Your buffalo robe?

                    MATTHEW
         That's right.

                    HAWK
         You kill buffalo today?

                    MATTHEW
         No. I never killed no buffalo.
         Never!

> HAWK
> Then where you get robe?

> MATTHEW
> (Beat; resentful)
> From a trader... 'bout a hundred miles back.

> BARKLEY
> (Tries to defuse situation)
> What's the problem, Hawk?

Hawk and Matthew's eyes remain locked.

> HAWK
> Buffalo slaughtered.... Meat rotting on prairie.... One day ride from here.

> MATTHEW
> I... I told you. I don't know nuthin' 'bout that.

> BARKLEY
> Hell, these ain't the people you want. There were a couple of fellas... nasty sorts... here earlier today. Had a wagon full of hides to trade.

Hawk turns his attention toward Barkley.

> BARKLEY
> (Continuing)
> You can follow their tracks west in the mornin'.

Both Rebecca and Matthew appear nonplussed at Barkley's betrayal of a fellow white man.

Hawk ponders a moment; accepts Barkley's statement. He turns back to Matthew; indicates the Henry.

>   HAWK
> Good rifle. You trade?

>   MATTHEW
> No.

>   HAWK
> Six ponies outside. Good ponies.

>   MATTHEW
> No!

Hawk tenses; scowls, as he grips the Henry. Spotted Face and Little Rabbit mutter a few words in Cheyenne.

Matthew starts to raise the Colt. Barkley, virtually reading Matthew's mind, steps between him and Hawk.

>   BARKLEY
>   (To Matthew)
> Hell, son, you gotta fight with everybody?
>   (Turns to Hawk)
> It belonged to his pa.

Hawk ponders; buys Barkley's rationalization. He nods; hands Barkley the rifle.

>   BARKLEY
>   (Continuing)
> Now, why don't you three sit
> down and fill your bellies.

Hawk and his two companions move to the table and sit.

                    BARKLEY
               (Continuing; to Rebecca)
          Ma'm, would you please give
          these warriors some of that
          delicious prairie stew?

Rebecca hesitates.

                    BARKLEY
               (Continuing)
          Go on. They won't hurt ya.

Uneasy, Rebecca takes the stew pot; brings it over to the table. The LIGHT hits her blonde hair, attracting the three Indians' attention. Hawk appears particularly taken with her.

                    MATTHEW
               (Whispers; to Barkley)
          I don't like my wife servin' no Indians.

Barkley, angrily, slams the Henry into Matthew's gut; pushes him back against the wall.

                    BARKLEY
               (Voice low)
          Look, boy... I knew you were dumb,
          but I didn't figure you to be the
          dumbest dummy east of the Rockies....
          If you ain't careful, pretty soon, yer
          gonna be so dumb, yer gonna be dead.
               (Beat)
          And, as far as yer wife's servin'
          Indjun's is concerned... Hawk is kin.
          He were my wife's cousin.

Barkley and a more somber Matthew watch Rebecca bring plates over to the Indians. She never looks directly at the Indians, but Hawk does not take his eyes off of her.

                                        CUT TO:

EXT. TRADING POST YARD. NIGHT.

Awhile later. Matthew, carrying his Henry, and Rebecca, with her buffalo robe, exit the building; head for their wagon. CAMERA TRACKS. Behind them, Barkley stands silhouetted in the doorway.

>   BARKLEY
> You folks sleep good, now.
> I'll talk to ya in the mornin'.

>   REBECCA
> Thank you, Mr. Barkley.

>   MATTHEW
>   (Tense; whispers
>   to Rebecca)
> I don't like this.

They continue toward their wagon.

CUT TO:

INT. TRADING POST. NIGHT.

The Indians, a bit more relaxed now that the Carvers have left, are still sitting around the table. Barkley walks back from the front door.

>   BARKLEY
> Nice couple. Wife's expectin'....
> Was thinkin' of lettin' 'em stay
> here 'til the first wagon train
> comes through next spring.

HAWK
               (Matter-of-fact)
            Man has much to learn.

Barkley moves behind the counter.

                   BARKLEY
            That's what scares me.
               (Produces whiskey
                jug from under
                counter.)
            Who's for a snort?

Hawk and his companions grin; nod approval. Spotted Face appears particularly pleased. Barkley brings the jug over to the table; sits with his longtime friends.

                   BARKLEY
               (Continuing)
            Had to wait 'til the youngsters
            left, otherwise they'd be tellin'
            folks I was givin' whiskey to the
            Indians.

Hawk chuckles at Barkley's joke; quickly translates it into Cheyenne for Spotted Face and Little Rabbit, and they also laugh. Barkley hands the jug to Little Rabbit, who only gets a short swig before Spotted Face reaches over and snatches it away from him.

                   BARKLEY
               (Continuing; to Hawk)
            So, what're ya gonna do when
            you catch up with them buffalo
            hunters tomorrow?

Spotted Face, finishing a long swig from the jug, apparently understands the gist of Barkley's question. He angrily draws his finger across his throat, indicating that the men will die.

> HAWK
> (Simply)
> No! Talk first. Then...we see.

Locking eyes with Spotted Face, he takes the jug from him; swallows from it.

> CUT TO:

INT. SCHOONER WAGON. NIGHT.

Matthew and Rebecca are bedding down for the night. Through the back of the wagon, he watches the front door of the building.

> MATTHEW
> I just don't like it! A white
> man sendin' Indians out to kill
> other whites.

> REBECCA
> (Annoyed)
> He was tryin' to help us, Matthew....
> Why are you so angry?

> MATTHEW
> You'd be angry, too, if that old
> geezer was callin' you dumb all
> the time....

> REBECCA
> Matthew....

> MATTHEW
> Yer my wife, Becky. Every time
> I look at yer face, you look like
> yer disappointed in me.

REBECCA
(Beat)
You promised me a home. A place of our own.

MATTHEW
I'm tryin'. I'm doin' my best....
I make mistakes just like everybody else.

REBECCA
(Sympathetic)
I know.... I was just hopin' fer somethin' better than what I had before.

He takes her in his arms; hugs her.

MATTHEW
Our son will have a good home, Becky. I promise you that.
(Beat)
I was thinkin'. Them fellas today....
Maybe they'd help us get across the mountains.

REBECCA
(Shakes head)
I didn't like them, Matthew.

MATTHEW
I didn't much neither. But, if I warn 'em 'bout them Indians, they're goin' to be beholdin' to us.

REBECCA
(Doubtful)
I don't know....

                    MATTHEW
          I know it's not right for whites
          to stand by and let other whites
          get slaughtered.

                    REBECCA
               (Beat)
          Why don't you sleep on it. See
          how things are in the morning.

                    MATTHEW
               (Cocking Henry)
          I'm not sleepin'. Keepin' an eye
          on them Indians.

He turns from her; continues to watch the building. Rebecca pulls the buffalo robe up over her; tries to sleep.

                                        DISSOLVE TO:

INT. SCHOONER WAGON. NIGHT.

Awhile later. Rebecca is asleep under the buffalo robe. Still holding the Henry, Matthew is dozing in a sitting position. SOUND of somebody urinating on the ground outside the wagon.

Suddenly, Matthew snaps awake; grips the rifle. He looks outside the wagon and sees:

Hawk, slightly inebriated, stands a few feet away from the wagon, urinating. He glances over at the startled Matthew, then back at the ground.

                    HAWK
               (Amused)
          No worry. Only scalp whites
          in daylight.

He finishes his business; walks back to the building.

An irked Matthew watches him enter.

CUT TO:

INT. SCHOONER WAGON. DAWN.

Rebecca, still asleep, is alone in the wagon.

EXT. TRADING POST YARD. DAWN.

Matthew is inside the corral, saddling one of Barkley's horses, a bay. He has the Henry with him.

EXT. TRADING POST YARD. DAWN.

Leading the horse, Matthew walks to the edge of the yard. Once there, he mounts the animal; heads off in the same direction that Kearney and Nielsen left the previous day.

CUT TO:

EXT. TRADING POST YARD. MORNING.

Barkley, Hawk, Little Rabbit and Spotted Face are near the corral. The trader is examining the string of ponies that the Indians had brought with them.

BARKLEY
Good horses.
(Beat)
Reminds me of the string I sold
last month to a buyer for the
Union Army.

HAWK
(Deadpan)
No ask. No worry.

> BARKLEY
> (Shrugs; hides amusement)
> Pick up yer supplies on the way back.

Hawk nods; mounts his horse.

INT. SCHOONER WAGON. MORNING.

Rebecca awakens; finds herself alone. She looks out of the wagon toward the corral and sees:

Barkley exchanging a few unintelligible words with the Indians, who then ride out of the yard, heading west.

As Hawk rides off, he throws a glance at Rebecca, who ducks down out of sight.

Barkley leads the string of ponies to the corral.

> CUT TO:

EXT. TRADING POST YARD. MORNING.

Ponies inside, Barkley shuts the corral; notes that something is amiss. He starts to count the horses. Behind him, Rebecca approaches from the schooner wagon.

> REBECCA
> 'Morning, Mr. Barkley.

> BARKLEY
> 'Morning, ma'm.

> REBECCA
> You seen my husband?

> BARKLEY
> (Beat)
> He's probably with my bay.

                    REBECCA
                (Startled)
          What!?!

                    BARKLEY
          Got a horse missin'.
                (Notes her concern)
          He probably just rode out fer
          a look-see. He'll be back soon.

                    REBECCA
          I can't imagine why....

                    BARKLEY
                (Interrupts)
          Like some breakfast? I flip a
          pretty good flapjack.

                    REBECCA
                (Putting her concern aside)
          That'd be nice. Thank you.

They walk toward the building.

                                        CUT TO:

EXT. THE PRAIRIE. MORNING.

Matthew, riding the bay, follows the wagon tracks west.

                                        CUT TO:

INT. TRADING POST. MORNING.

Barkley is at the stove, skillet in hand, making his flapjacks. During the following, Rebecca clears and sets the table.

                    BARKLEY
          Been awhile since I had a woman around.

                    REBECCA
            (Brushing dust from
            the table)
Yes.

                    BARKLEY
When's the young'un due?

                    REBECCA
Before Spring.
            (Beat)
You and your... wife.... You didn't
have any children?

                    BARKLEY
One boy. Three years old when the
fever took 'im.
            (Beat)
Hell, the fever'll take the whole
damned country if folks ain't careful.
            (Embarrassed)
Sorry, ma'm.

He flips a flapjack.

                    REBECCA
            (Looks toward door)
I hope Matthew is all right.

                    BARKLEY
If he's not back in awhile, I'll
ride out and look fer 'im.

                    REBECCA
            (Beat)
Mr. Barkley.... Can I ask you somethin'?

                    BARKLEY
You go right ahead.

                    REBECCA
                (Hesitant)
            Matthew was wonderin'.... Last
            night, you told them Indians which
            way them buffalo hunters went.

                    BARKLEY
            So?

                    REBECCA
            They were <u>white</u> men.

                    BARKLEY
            Hawk'd found the tracks this
            morning anyway.
                (Beat)
            If you want to get along out here,
            ma'm, you don't tell lies to no Indians.

Rebecca continues at the table; avoids his eyes.

                    BARKLEY
                (Continuing)
            Somethin' you might be wantin'
            to tell me, ma'm?

                    REBECCA
            No.... No, I was just wonderin'....

Again, she throws a worried glance toward the door. Barkley looks at her; ponders.

                                            CUT TO:

EXT. THE PRAIRIE. DAY.

Matthew continues to follow the wagon tracks.

                                            CUT TO:

EXT. ANOTHER PART OF THE PRAIRIE. DAY.

The Indians have momentarily stopped in their pursuit of the wagon. Hawk and Spotted Face sit on their ponies, as Little Rabbit examines the ground. (NOTE: Dialogue in quotations are spoken in the Cheyenne language, or in certain later scenes, Pawnee, and sub-titled on the screen in English.)

>   LITTLE RABBIT
>   "Another rider follows the wagon."

Hawk and Spotted Face exchange a curious look. Little Rabbit remounts and the trio proceed on their way.

>   CUT TO:

EXT. THE PRAIRIE. DAY.

Matthew reaches the top of a rise. About a half mile away, he spots Kearney and Nielsen's campsite.

EXT. CAMPSITE. DAY.

The men are breaking camp, but there is still coffee on the fire. Nielsen packs up bedrolls and other belongings, while Kearney hitches the horses to the wagon. Nielsen glances up; gazes into the distance.

>   NIELSEN
>   Got company.
>
>   KEARNEY
>   (Squints)
>   So we do.

Both men take up their rifles; move closer to the wagon, as they watch the distant figure of Matthew ride toward them.

EXT. THE PRAIRIE. DAY.

CAMERA TRACKS Matthew, as he rides up to the campsite. The Henry is across his lap.

Cradling their rifles, Kearney and Nielsen step out from the wagon to meet him.

>   KEARNEY
>   (Jocular)
> Well, what a surprise! And, what would we be owin' to this mornin's visit?

>   MATTHEW
> There're three Cheyenne behind me... trailing your wagon. I don't know how far back.

>   KEARNEY
> Oh?

>   MATTHEW
> They came lookin' for buffalo hunters last night. Barkley, the trader, pointed them after you.

Kearney throws a glance at Nielsen.

>   KEARNEY
>   (To Matthew)
> He did, did he?
>   (Beat; lowers rifle)
> Well, I'm thankin' you for the warnin'.

Kearney eyes the Henry on Matthew's lap.

                    MATTHEW
               (Beat; relaxes)
          My wife and I was hopin' we could
          join you crossin' the mountains.

Kearney throws another glance at Nielsen, who also lowers his weapon.

                    KEARNEY
               (Indicates campfire)
          Would you like a cup of coffee?

                    MATTHEW
          Thank you.

Matthew gets ready to dismount.

                    KEARNEY
          I sure do admire that Henry.

Kearney, suddenly, raises his rifle; FIRES once at Matthew.

The bullet hits Matthew square between the eyes. His expression is one of total surprise, as he topples off his horse.

Kearney retrieves the Henry from the ground. He beams a grin at Nielsen.

                                        WIPE TO:

EXT. THE PRAIRIE. DAY.

Awhile later. Hawk, Spotted Face and Little Rabbit reach the top of a hill; rein their horses. About a half mile ahead of them, they see:

The Kearney/Nielsen wagon heads slowly toward the mountains.

Two men, indistinguishable at this distance, sit on the front seat. The bay is tied to the back of the conveyance.

Hawk studies the wagon, then gestures to his companions. The Indians move forward, riding abreast of each other with Hawk in the center. They keep several yards between them.

THE WAGON

The wagon moves slowly forward, with an anxious Nielsen at the reins. Next to him on the seat is the lifeless body of Matthew, tied in a sitting position.

In the distance, behind them, the Indians come riding down the hill; head toward the wagon.

> KEARNEY (O.S.)
> Here they come.

Kearney lies flat in the back of the wagon, peeking over the top. He holds the Henry, ready to fire.

> NIELSEN
> Just... just don't miss.

> KEARNEY
> Otto, me boy, I was the best
> shot in the county.

THE PLAIN

The Indians begin to close the distance, branching off so that Spotted Face and Little Rabbit ultimately ride abreast of the wagon, while Hawk stays about fifty yards behind it. They make no move to attack, simply keep pace with the conveyance.
CAMERA TRACKS.

THE WAGON

Nielsen's anxiety is approaching panic. He shouts over his shoulder to Kearney.

> NIELSEN
> Jesus Christ! Do somethin'!

Kearney, suddenly, raises up; FIRES TWICE at Little Rabbit.

The Indian is hit in the chest with both bullets. He pitches off his horse onto the ground.

Frightened, Nielsen joggles the reins.

> NIELSEN
> (Shouts at horses)
> Hi-yah!

THE PLAIN

The wagon moves faster across the flat land.

Hawk and Spotted Face are caught by surprise. They momentarily rein their ponies. Hawk rides over to where Little Rabbit has fallen; dismounts and checks the lifeless body of his friend. The sorrow in his face quickly turns to an expression of anger. He exchanges a glance with Spotted Face. Both men know what they must do.

Hawk remounts, and the two Indians start after the fleeing wagon.

THE WAGON

Kearney takes aim at Hawk, who, musket in hand, is moving up on the wagon. Just as the Irishman FIRES, the wagon hits a bump and his shot goes wild.

                    KEARNEY
               (Shouts at Nielsen)
          Slow down. I can't get a shot.

                    NIELSEN
               (Over his shoulder)
          You slow down!

Another bump, and Kearney loses his balance. He tumbles back onto the wagon floor.

THE PLAIN

His pony in full gallop, Spotted Face nears the side of the wagon. Bow and arrow in hand he takes aim; shoots an arrow.

THE WAGON

The arrow hits the upright body of Matthew in the back of the neck.

THE PLAIN

Galloping up on the opposite side of the wagon from Spotted Face, Hawk raises his musket; FIRES.

THE WAGON

Nielsen is hit in the back.

                    NIELSEN
               (Screams in pain)
          Shit!

He drops the reins, which fall down between the racing team of horses.

THE PLAIN

Hawk is moving up fast on the wagon.

THE WAGON

Kearney does not see Hawk approach. His attention is on the opposite side of the wagon. In a sitting position, he aims the Henry at Spotted Face; FIRES.

The Indian takes a mortal wound; pitches off his pony.

Kearney turns; gets ready to fire at Hawk.

THE PLAIN

Hawk leaps from his pony onto the wagon, tackling Kearney. Both men tumble out of the wagon.
The out-of-control wagon hits another bump; turns over.

Nielsen is pitched hard onto the ground. His head hits a large rock and he lies still.

Several yards away, both Hawk and Kearney are momentarily stunned from their violent fall.

Hawk is the first to struggle to his feet. His right leg will not support him, broken in the fall. He tumbles backward onto the ground.

Raising himself up to a sitting position, Kearney shakes his head to clear it. He spots Hawk, again trying to get to his feet.

Hawk makes it up to a half kneeling position. His eyes lock onto Kearney's. He reaches for his Bowie knife.

Kearney grabs the Colt out of his belt; FIRES TWICE at Hawk. The Indian is hit. He falls backward onto the ground, and does not move.

The Irishman gets to his feet; surveys his surroundings. The wagon has overturned. The team of horses and the bay stand about fifty yards away. Nielsen lies a few feet from the wagon.

Kearney strolls over to the wagon. The Henry lies nearby. Kearney beams; picks up the rifle.

>   KEARNEY
>   And here I thought I'd lost you,
>   my darlin'.

He does a quick little Irish jig, then looks over at Nielsen's body. CAMERA TRACKS, as he strolls over to it.

>   KEARNEY
>   (To the body;
>   disdainful)
>   Otto, me boy, you are so damn
>   inconsiderate.... Leavin' me all
>   alone out here to dig a grave for
>   your bloody ass.

He spits onto the ground.

                                        DISSOLVE TO:

EXT. TRADING POST YARD. DAY.

Rebecca emerges from the building, broom in hand, sweeping the dirt she has collected from inside out into the yard. She pauses for a moment; looks off in the direction of the wagon tracks. A expression of concern crosses her face, as she takes the broom back inside.

                                        CUT TO:

EXT. THE PRAIRIE. DAY.

A WIND is blowing across the prairie, causing a mild dust storm. CAMERA PANS, and we can make out the overturned wagon, scattered supplies, Spotted Face's body and a hastily dug and covered shallow grave.

CAMERA MOVES IN on the still form of Hawk, his leg twisted; his face and shirt covered in blood. In the distance, we HEAR the sound of horses approaching.

CLOSE SHOT

Light dust blows over Hawk's face. He stirs; tries to open his eyes. The dust makes it difficult. Then, a canteen is pressed to his mouth and a hand reaches under his head, lifting him up to drink. Eagerly, he gulps the water.

      BARKLEY (O.S.)
  Not so fast.

BACK TO SCENE

Barkley kneels next to the injured Indian. He restrains his attempts to rise.

      HAWK
    (Somewhat disoriented)
  My.... My brothers!?!

      BARKLEY
  Jest take it easy. There's
  nuthin' you can do fer them.
    (Surveys scene)
  Christ, Hawk... What the hell
  happened?

          CUT TO:

EXT. TRADING POST YARD. DUSK.

A cold wind is blowing. SOUND of horses approaching.

INT. TRADING POST. DUSK.

The stove is lit; the door shut. The place is much cleaner, neater than when we last saw it.

Apprehensive; trying to keep busy, Rebecca lights the oil lamps. She keeps glancing at the door. She freezes; stops what she's doing when she hears the SOUND of horses. Then, HEAVY FOOTSTEPS on the wooden porch. Almost afraid to move, she stares at the door.

Suddenly, the door slams open, revealing Kearney, covered with dust. He carries the Henry at his side.

Rebecca gasps; backs up a few steps.

Kearney beams his roguish smile.

> KEARNEY
> Good evenin' to ya, ma'm.

He enters; slams the door behind him. Rebecca doesn't move.

> KEARNEY
> (Continuing)
> You needn't be frightened of me.
> I just want to get out of the cold.
> (Spots stove)
> Mind if I make use of yer stove?

Without waiting for her to reply, Kearney strolls to the back of the room; warms himself at the stove.

KEARNEY
(Continuing; looks
about)
Where's Barkley?

REBECCA
(Beat)
He went looking for....
(Notices Henry)
Where.... Where is my husband?

KEARNEY
Yer husband?
(Beat)
Yer husband was a good man, m'am.
Risked his own life to warn us.

REBECCA
(Terrified)
Was!?!

KEARNEY
(Nods)
I'm afraid the bloody Indians
killed 'im, m'am.
(Points to back of
his neck)
Arrow.... Killed my partner,
too.

Rebecca is stunned; speechless.

KEARNEY
(Continuing)
I brought yer husband's body
back, ma'm. So, you can bury
'im proper.

REBECCA
                (Softly; to herself)
            No....
                    (Screams)
            NO!

Rebecca faints onto the floor. Kearney doesn't move; just stares at her.

                    KEARNEY
            And why would you be gettin' so
            upset?

He shrugs; continues to warm himself.

                                    DISSOLVE TO:

EXT. TRADING POST YARD. NIGHT.

The cold wind continues to blow.

INT. TRADING POST. NIGHT.

Rebecca sits at the table, weeping. Kearney, feigning concern, brings her a cup of coffee from the stove.

                    REBECCA
                (Suppressing anger; to
                herself)
            I told him not to go.... Why did
            he always have to prove something?

Kearney sits at the table; takes a bottle of whiskey from his coat pocket and pours a shot into the cup.

                    KEARNEY
            Drink that, ma'm.

                    REBECCA
            (Takes cup)
        What is it?

                    KEARNEY
        Good ol' American coffee... with
        a shot of the good ol' Irish.

Rebecca hesitates.

                    KEARNEY
            (Continuing)
        It'll make you feel better.

Rebecca wipes her eyes; looks at Kearney, wanting...needing to trust him... someone. She gulps down the liquid; coughs.

                    KEARNEY
            (Chuckles)
        Like a real colleen.

                    REBECCA
        I.... I never tasted whiskey
        before.

                    KEARNEY
        Life's full of new experiences.

                    REBECCA
            (Beat)
        Mr. Kearney.... I got a baby
        comin'.

                    KEARNEY
        No family?

REBECCA
                 (Shakes head)
            I was a servant girl on this
            farm back in Massachusetts.
            Matthew'd run away after his
            pa died. Said he was tired of his
            step-father whippin' 'im. He was
            workin' for a neighbor... tryin' to
            avoid the conscription... when we....
                 (Muses)
            We took to each other right away.
            He was strong, handsome... curly hair....
                 (Burst of anger)
            He said we'd have our own place
            in Oregon.
                 (Weeps)
            What am I gonna do?

                    KEARNEY
            Now, don't be so hard on the lad.
            He was a good man.... You know the
            last thing he said as he lay dyin'
            in me arms?

                    REBECCA
            What?

                    KEARNEY
            "Kearney," he said.... "Take care
            my Becky fer me. She's gonna need
            a man to look after 'er."

Rebecca looks at Kearney. She'd like to believe him, but somehow she doesn't.

                    BARKLEY (O.S.)
          Ain't that touchin'.

Startled, Rebecca and Kearney turn to see:

Barkley stands in the open doorway, shivering from the cold. He carries his rifle at the ready. He kicks the door shut with his foot.

                    REBECCA
          Mr. Barkley!

                    KEARNEY
          The renegade trader!

Kearney's eyes travel to the Henry. It's across the room... lying on the counter... closer to Barkley than him.

                    BARKLEY
                    (Angry)
          Renegade!?!

He points the rifle at Kearney; stalks toward him.

                    BARKLEY
                    (Continuing)
          You dirty murderin' scum!

Kearney's hand moves toward the Colt in his belt.

                    BARKLEY
                    (Continuing)
          Keep yer hands on the table.

Kearney obeys. Barkley moves closer; turns to Rebecca who's totally perplexed at what's happening.

                    BARKLEY
                 (Continuing)
            What'd he tell ya, ma'm? That
            the Indians killed yer husband?

Rebecca nods.

                    BARKLEY
                 (Continuing)
            He's a liar! Ask 'im how come
            there's a bullet hole right between
            yer man's eyes.

Rebecca looks questioningly over at Kearney. After a moment, the Irishman shrugs; guffaws.

                    KEARNEY
            He had 'im a fine rifle.... Fine woman, too.

Suddenly, Rebecca explodes with a fury one would've never thought was within her. She screams; throws herself at Kearney... beating on and scratching at his face.

Recovering quickly from his surprise, the powerful Kearney grabs her; rises from his seat. He spins her around; holds her in front of him.

Barkley isn't sure what to do. He can't fire without hitting Rebecca.

Kearney holds Rebecca with one arm, and grabs his Colt with his free hand. He FIRES TWICE at Barkley.

Barkley is hit. He stumbles backwards; falls onto his back. His rifle FIRES into the ceiling.

Rebecca screams. She breaks away from the Irishman's grasp; races for the door.

Kearney rushes forward; hesitates next to Barkley. As Rebecca opens the front door, Kearney FIRES a final round into the old trader.

A blast of cold air hits the Irishman in the face. He glances up in time to see Rebecca disappear through the door and out into the night.

>   KEARNEY
>   (Chuckles to himself;
>   shrugs)
>   Guess I'm gonna have to do it the
>   hard way.

He heads for the door, grabbing the Henry off the counter as he goes.

EXT. TRADING POST YARD. NIGHT.

Kearney emerges from the building; stands on the porch, silhouetted in the doorway. He looks about.

>   KEARNEY
>   (Calls; amused)
>   Now why would you want to be out
>   here freezin' yerself to death?

Underneath the open porch steps, a frightened Rebecca keeps very still.

>   KEARNEY (O.S.)
>   (Continuing; calls)
>   You can never tell what kinda
>   goblins are gonna getcha on such
>   a black night.

Kearney starts down the steps. Halfway down, he stops; listens.

                    KEARNEY
               (Continuing; calls)
          Becky, my darlin', you're out
          here all alone. You are gonna
          need a man to look after ya.

Rebecca tries not to breathe. She moves further back under the porch. Through the steps, she watches Kearney descend to the ground.

                    KEARNEY (O.S.)
               (Continuing; to himself)
          Ah, the trouble you women put me through....
          But yer worth it...most of the time.

He strolls off into the darkness.

Rebecca doesn't move. She listens. Silence. Slowly, she crawls out from her hiding place. She looks up, and sees:

The door to the building is still open.

Getting to her feet, Rebecca starts to move around to the front of the steps.

                    KEARNEY (O.S.)
          Wondered when you'd be out.

Rebecca spins around. Kearney is standing right behind her, grinning like a Cheshire cat. He drops the Henry; grabs both her arms and pulls her toward him.

                    KEARNEY
               (Continuing)
          Ain't it time you got a bit friendlier.

He presses his mouth against hers. She tries to resist, but he's much too strong for her.

                    KEARNEY
              (Continuing; chuckles)
         A wildcat!

He starts to paw at her clothes, when, suddenly, we HEAR a THUD.

A look of total shock crosses Kearney's face. He pitches forward, face down onto the ground. Rebecca grabs onto the porch steps to prevent her falling over with him. She looks down at the Irishman and sees:

A Bowie knife is buried deep in his back.

Rebecca gasps; looks up.

Hawk limps out of the darkness. He is very weak. A crude splint is on his leg; improvised bandages on his bare chest and forehead. His expression, however, is one of satisfaction. He stares down at the man that he has just killed, then at Rebecca.

Rebecca's emotions are mixed, confusion... fright. She'd like to scream, but....

Hawk's leg gives out from under him. He collapses onto the ground, unconscious.

Rebecca hesitates, then comprehending what has happened, moves over to the Indian. Tentatively, she kneels next to him; feels his forehead.

Shivering from the cold, she looks about; spots the water barrel near the porch. She hurries over to the barrel; grabs and fills the pitcher on top of it, then rushes back to the unconscious Indian.

She pours some water onto his face. Hawk opens his eyes; looks up at her, dazed.

                    REBECCA
            You're gonna freeze out here.

She starts to tug on his arm.
                    REBECCA
                    (Continuing)
            I can't get you inside by
            myself.

Hawk nods; allows Rebecca to help him to his feet. She puts his arm around her shoulder.

                    HAWK
            You no afraid?

                    REBECCA
            I'm scared to death.

She helps Hawk as he stumbles over to the steps; grabs onto the railing. She continues to support him up the stairs and into the building.

                                        DISSOLVE TO:

INT. TRADING POST. DAWN.

Barkley's body has been removed. CAMERA DOLLYS past the counter to the back of the store, where we discover Hawk, ill, delirious, lying on the bed. He is naked to the waist. His wounds are open, so that hot compresses can be applied directly to them. To keep it immobile, his broken leg has been tied to the bedpost, as have his hands and other leg.

Rebecca, looking drawn, tired, sits next to the bed in the rocking chair, dozing. A pot of water boils on the stove.

Hallucinating and drenched with perspiration, Hawk mumbles some words in Cheyenne.

Rebecca awakens, momentarily unsure of her surroundings. She sees that Hawk is having problems; goes to him and puts her hand on his forehead. Then, using a stick to carry it, she takes a hot rag from the boiling water; puts it on the Indian's wound. He does not react to the heat.

From a bucket on the floor next to the bed, she takes a cold wet cloth; places it on Hawk's forehead.

Rebecca watches him; appears concerned. After a moment, she glances toward the door. There is something she must do.

CUT TO:

EXT. TRADING POST YARD. DAY.

Several yards from the trading post building, a large mound of dirt sits atop a freshly covered mass grave.

Rebecca, exhausted and covered in perspiration, pats down the top of the mound with a shovel. Then, still holding the shovel, she plops down onto the ground. She sits spread-legged, staring at the mound. After a moment, she speaks to the grave.

                  REBECCA
        (Matter-of-fact)
You were always a mess of work,
weren't ya, Matthew?
        (Beat)
Well, you still are.... Sorry I had to
stick ya in there with Mr. Barkley and
that no good that done you in, but, dang
it, Matthew, it was a lot o' hard work
diggin' one hole... let alone three of 'em.
        (Her eyes become moist)
I don't wanna lose our baby, Matthew.
That's all that's gonna be left of you here.
        (Irked)
                         (more)

                    REBECCA (Cont'd)
          'Lot you care! Go off an' get yerself
          killed. Leave me to raise 'im alone.
                    (Beat)
          I got an' Indian in there with a bullet
          in 'im that's probably gonna die on me....
          An', if he lives, he'll probably wind
          up rapin' me an' makin' me his squaw.
                    ((Shouts at grave)
          Hope it's pretty darn hot wherever you
          are, Matthew!
                    (Sobs)
          No.... No, you were a good man....
          Tried to be a good husband.
                    (Beat)
          But, Mr. Barkley <u>was</u> right. You <u>were</u>
          kinda dumb.
                    (Beat)
          Wherever you are now, you just better
          listen to him. He'll keep you outta trouble.

Rebecca wipes her eyes. With the help of the shovel, she gets to her feet.

                    REBECCA
                    (Continuing)
          I gotta go, now. See if that
          Indian's still breathin'....
          'Bye, Matthew.

She starts to turn away from the grave, then:

                    REBECCA
                    (Continuing; looks skyward)
          Amen.

Rebecca walks back to the building.
                                        CUT TO:

INT. TRADING POST. DAY.

Rebecca is at Hawk's bedside, wiping the perspiration from his chest with a dry cloth. She examines his open, still festering wound.

Suddenly, Hawk's eyes open.

Rebecca is startled; moves back a step.

Dazed, the Indian glowers at her for a moment, then realizes that his limbs are tied to the bedposts. He starts to struggle.

                  HAWK
        Why... why you tie me?

                REBECCA
        You got a broken leg. You can't
        move it if you want it to set proper.

He stops struggling.

                  HAWK
        (Beat)
        Hands not broken.

Rebecca is hesitant to untie him.

                REBECCA
        (Beat)
        Mr. Hawk.... You got a bullet
        in you. If it don't come out...
        you're gonna die.

                  HAWK
        Me <u>no</u> die! Untie hands!
        Go see medicine man.

                        REBECCA
            Mr. Hawk.... You couldn't sit
            a horse with that leg.

                        HAWK
                 (Shouts; struggles)
            Untie hands!

Ignoring him, Rebecca walks to the counter. CAMERA TRACKS.

                        REBECCA
            I held a lamp for a doctor once. Saw
            him take a bullet out of a man's leg.
            Didn't look too hard...
                    (To herself)
            ...for the doctor.

During the following, she gets Barkley's whiskey jug from behind the counter, smells the contents, then brings it back to Hawk.

                        REBECCA
                     (Continuing)
            I don't know what exactly's in this here
            jug, but if it's anything like what that
            doctor gave his patient before he started
            diggin', you ain't gonna feel much.

                        HAWK
                      (Shouts)
            Untie hands!!

He is too weak to continue struggling.

                        REBECCA
                    (Hands on hips)
            You gonna drink this, or am I gonna
            have to pour it down ya?

Hawk curses her in his native tongue.

                              REBECCA
                   They never taught ya not to talk
                   that way in front of a lady, huh?

She sits on the side of the bed, lifts his head and starts to pour the liquor into his mouth. Reluctantly, he swallows.

                                                    CUT TO:

INT. TRADING POST. DAY.

Several minutes later. Hawk lies on the bed, drunkenly chanting a Cheyenne war song.

Rebecca is at the stove, heating a knife over the open flame. Ready, she turns to the Indian, who beams a tight grin at her; continues to chant. As she crosses toward the bed:

                              REBECCA
                            (To herself)
                   Girl, you'd better do this right.

                                                    CUT TO:

EXT. TRADING POST YARD. DAY.

From inside the building, we HEAR Hawk's chanting. The intensity of the chant increases. A sharp cry of pain. Silence.

The cold wind blows over the mass grave.

                                                    FADE OUT.

FADE IN:

INT. TRADING POST. DAY.

From Hawk's P.O.V., we see Rebecca standing over the bed, holding a small wooden bowl and spoon. She looks tired.

                    REBECCA
            You feelin' better?

Hawk does not answer. He simply studies her; his expression giving no clue to his thoughts. He lies flat on his back, his chest bandaged; limbs still tied to the bedposts. From the chest down, he is covered with a blanket.

                    REBECCA
                  (Continuing)
            You been out for two days.
                  (Sits next to bed)
            Thought I was gonna lose you
            last night.

Hawk maintains his gaze on her.

                    REBECCA
                  (Continuing; offers
                  bowl)
            Hungry?

A moment, then Hawk nods. His eyes shift to his right hand tied to the bedpost.

                    REBECCA
                  (Continuing; hesitant)
            Your... Your leg ain't set yet.
            You gotta stay still.

She holds out a spoonful of broth. He turns his head, refuses to let her feed him.

                    REBECCA
                  (Continuing)
            It's good broth.

He continues to ignore her.

                    REBECCA
              (Continuing; fearful)
        I... I can't untie you. I....

                     HAWK
              (Weak, but defiant)
        Me no move! Me no rape! Me just eat!

They stare at each other for a long moment. She believes him; cautiously unties his hands.

Hawk rubs his wrists, then, with some pain, reaches out for the bowl. She hands it to him, and he drinks hungrily from it. Finishing, he looks at her.

                    REBECCA
        More?

Hawk nods. She takes the bowl from him; goes to the stove for a refill.

Hawk suddenly becomes aware that he is naked under the blanket.

                     HAWK
                 (Startled)
        Where... Where clothes!?!

The question embarrasses Rebecca, but keeping her back turned toward the stove, she plows through.

                    REBECCA
        Washed 'em.... Had to wash you,
        too.

She crosses back to the bed, refusing to look directly at him. He takes the bowl from her.

                    REBECCA
                  (Continuing)
            Didn't like it any more than you.

She picks up a rusted metal chamber-like pot from under the bed; shows it to him.

                    REBECCA
                  (Continuing)
            You know how to use one of these,
            don't you?

Dropping it onto the bed, she turns and tromps away. Hawk stares after her, his expression betraying mild amusement.

                                        CUT TO:

EXT. TRADING POST YARD. DUSK.

A cold wind is blowing. Rebecca, a blanket wrapped around her shoulders, leads two horses toward the lean-to.

                                        CUT TO:

INT. LEAN-TO. DUSK.

All of the horses and both oxen are tied inside the flimsy structure. Using a pitchfork, Rebecca feeds them cut grass. She pauses momentarily; stretches her back muscles.

                                        CUT TO:

INT. TRADING POST. NIGHT.

It's suppertime. Rebecca sits at the table, eating her meal with Barkley's crude utensils. Across the room, leaning up on one elbow in the bed, Hawk eats his food with his fingers. He appears much stronger than when we last saw him. The pair eat in silence, each never taking their eyes off the other. Then:

                    REBECCA
        Mr. Hawk....

Hawk grunts acknowledgement.

                    REBECCA
                    (Continuing)
        Ain't yer tribe gonna be lookin' for
        you?

                    HAWK
                    (Shakes head)
        Me... my brothers... gone near two
        moons. Visit our cousins, the Arapaho.

Rebecca takes another bite of food, then:

                    REBECCA
                    (Beat)
        What about white settlers? Are there
        any in these parts?

                    HAWK
        Was. One family. Two day's ride.

                    REBECCA
        Was?

                    HAWK
        Pawnee burn house. They go.

Rebecca blanches. Silence for a few more moments.

                    HAWK
                    (Continuing)
        Where you go, now?

                    REBECCA
What?

                    HAWK
Man dead. Where you go?

                    REBECCA
Next wagon train. I'll join up
with them.

                    HAWK
Whites no come 'til Spring.

                    REBECCA
          (Surprised)
Spring!?!
          (Beat)
There's plenty of food... firewood
here....

                    HAWK
What you do when child come?

                    REBECCA
          (Pensive)
I... I ain't figured that out
yet.

                    HAWK
          (Beat)
You good woman. Not too smart...
but good.

He returns to his eating, as she stares at him, realizing the truth of her situation.

                              CUT TO:

EXT. TRADING POST YARD. DAY.

The sky is clear; the air crisp. Rebecca, a shawl around her shoulders, assists Hawk outside onto the porch. He wears a "white man's" shirt and pants, presumably culled from Matthew's scant wardrobe. His leg still housed in a splint, the Indian utilizes a crudely fashioned crutch to move about.

                REBECCA
    I don't think this is such a
    good idea.

                HAWK
    Tired of bed.

He leans his weight against the wall.

                REBECCA
    You might fall.
                HAWK
    I no fall.

Rebecca starts back inside.

                REBECCA
    I'll get you a chair.

                HAWK
    No chair! I walk. Good for
    leg.

He limps away from the wall; takes a step toward the stairs. Unaccustomed to the crutch, his leg gives out. He starts to stumble. Rebecca quickly rushes to him; prevents his falling. As she supports his weight on her shoulder, he looks at her.

HAWK
                (Continuing; beat)
            Get chair.

She leans him back against the wall; goes inside the trading post. A moment later, she returns with a chair and helps him to it.

                    HAWK
                (Sits)
            Tomorrow I walk.

He peers out across the river, into the distance.

                    REBECCA
            You want some coffee?

Without looking at her, Hawk grunts a "Yes." Rebecca, again, retreats into the building; returns with two cups. She lowers herself down onto the porch next to him; follows his eyes out into the distance. After a moment:

                    REBECCA
            What're you lookin' at?

                    HAWK
            I look at my people on way to
            winter camp. I should be with them.

                    REBECCA
                (Beat)
            You got a family, Mr. Hawk?

                    HAWK
                (Nods)
            Mother.

                    REBECCA
            No wife?

                    HAWK
          No have time for wife.

Again, Rebecca follows his eyes into the distance.

                    REBECCA
               (Beat)
          Mr. Barkley said you could be a
          chief some day.

                    HAWK
          Already chief. <u>Warrior</u> chief. Other
          chiefs will decide if I join them in
          tribal Council.

                    REBECCA
          Will they?

                    HAWK
          Maybe. Maybe not. Their thoughts...
          my thoughts... not always agree.

                    REBECCA
               (Beat)
          Like what?

                    HAWK
          Not Too Smart Woman ask many questions.

                    REBECCA
          I gotta talk to somebody.

                    HAWK
               (Beat)
          There are some among my people
          who agree with our enemy, the Pawnee.
          They say we should kill the white man.
          Destroy him before he destroys Cheyenne.

                    REBECCA
But, the white man ain't hurtin'
you. Most of 'em are like my
husband and me. Just passin' through
on our way to Oregon.

                    HAWK
Now you pass through. When great war
between whites in East over, more
whites will come. They will stay on
Cheyenne land. They will kill Cheyenne
buffalo. My people will go hungry.

                    REBECCA
No....

                    HAWK
My brother, Spotted Face, who is now
with the Wise One Above, said the Cheyenne
was like the mountain lion. He attack
all who pass through his territory....
I agree with him, except, I say, that
maybe the white man is like the grizzly
bear. He is stronger, and like the
grizzly's paws, his weapons are more
powerful.... Mountain lion wise. He
no attack the grizzly bear. He learns
to avoid him.

He sips his coffee; gazes out into the distance. Rebecca stares at him, somewhat impressed. After a moment:

                    HAWK
                (Continuing; not looking
                at her; deadpan, but with
                a mischievous glint in his eye)
Unless white man is buffalo hunter.
Then he no better than dog.
We eat <u>him</u> like dogs in our village.

                    REBECCA
            You.... You eat little dogs!?!

                     HAWK
            Big dogs, too. Taste good.

                    REBECCA
            That.... That's terrible!

                     HAWK
            No terrible! You find me dog.
            I cook it for you. You like.

                    REBECCA
                  (On her feet)
            If I ever get me a dog, you
            keep your dirty hands off it.

She stomps back into the trading post.

                    REBECCA (O.S.)
                  (Continuing; shouts)
            Disgusting!

Hawk chuckles to himself.

                                        DISSOLVE TO:

EXT. TRADING POST YARD. DAY.

Dark clouds fill the sky, as rain pounds into the earth, turning it into mud.

Through the rain, in the distance, we observe the vague silhouettes of four riders approaching the trading post.

INT. TRADING POST. DAY.

The hard rain beats down onto the roof. Several pots are set around the room to catch the water that is leaking through. The stove is lit, providing heat for the room.

Rebecca sits in the rocking chair, mending a blouse. Hawk walks back and forth across the store, exercising his splinted leg. He is becoming quite proficient with his crutch.

> REBECCA
> (Glances up from mending)
> You're gettin' pretty good with that crutch.

Hawk grunts agreement.

> REBECCA
> (Continuing)
> Maybe when the rain lets up, you could bring in some more firewood?

Hawk continues to walk.

> HAWK
> (Does not look at her)
> Cheyenne warrior no bring firewood.

> REBECCA
> (Incredulous)
> What!?!

> HAWK
> Woman's job get firewood. Bring water, too.

> REBECCA
> (Irked)
> Not where I come from, buster. What kind of gentleman are you?

                    HAWK
               (Matter-of-fact)
          Not Too Smart Woman have much to learn.

He continues to walk.

                    REBECCA
               (Angry)
          Stop callin' me that! My name
          is Rebecca. Mrs. Carver to <u>you</u>.

Hawk suddenly stops walking; listens.

                    REBECCA
               (Continuing)
          What is it?

Hawk holds up his hand, signaling her to be still. She obeys.

                    HAWK
          Riders come.

Rebecca freezes. They both listen, but the SOUND of the pounding rain dominates.

                    HAWK
               (Continuing)
          Four.

                    REBECCA
          I don't hear nothin'.

                    HAWK
               (Moves cautiously toward door.)
          Not Too Smart Mrs. Carver no
          have ear of Cheyenne warrior.
               (Listens at door)
          Indian ponies.
               (With distaste; hate)
          Pawnee.

                    REBECCA
               (On her feet;
               frightened)
          Pawnee!?! Why not Cheyenne?

Hawk throws a hard glance at her.

                    REBECCA
               (Continuing)
          What... What do we do!?!

Hawk grabs the Henry off the counter; hobbles toward the rear door.

                    HAWK
          You talk.

He unbars the rear door.

                    REBECCA
          And you?

                    HAWK
          I no here.

Grasping the Henry, he exits through the rear, shutting the door behind him.

Rebecca appears anxious; momentarily at a loss. She moves around to behind the counter. Concealed beneath the counter is a revolver. Her hand brushes against it, as she faces the front door.

                                        CUT TO:

EXT. TRADING POST YARD. DAY.

Rain is coming down in torrents. Its SOUND is almost deafening.

Moving as quickly as possible, Hawk hobbles on his crutch from the rear of the building over to behind the schooner wagon. CAMERA TRACKS.

Four Pawnee braves ride into the yard of the trading post. The leader is RED KNIFE, 30, a husky warrior with a nasty disposition. He is accompanied by MOLE ON THE FACE, 25, who wears a large birthmark on his cheek; IRON BEAR, 20, a 6 foot robust warrior, and OWL EYES, 18, a young, hot-tempered brave. All four men have front-loading muskets; speak in the Pawnee language.

                    RED KNIFE
                (To Iron Bear and Owl
                    Eyes)
            "Wait outside. Look around"

Red Knife and Mole on the Face dismount; walk up onto the porch.

Behind the schooner wagon, Hawk takes aim at Red Knife with the Henry; decides not to fire.

As Iron Bear and Owl Eyes dismount, Red Knife and Mole on the Face enter the building.

INT. TRADING POST. DAY.

The door slams open, and Red Knife and Mole on the Face enter, dripping wet. Both warriors carry their muskets at the ready.

There expressions are mean; nasty.

Rebecca gasps; grips the revolver under the counter.

The Indians are surprised, pleased to see Rebecca.

EXT. TRADING POST YARD. DAY.

Hawk watches from behind the schooner wagon, as Iron Bear and Owl Eyes, muskets ready, head over to the lean-to; check the animals inside. They mutter something unintelligible in Pawnee.

Staying behind the wagon, Hawk maneuvers around so that he can observe the front entrance to the trading post building. The door is open, but he cannot see inside.

INT. TRADING POST. DAY.

Rebecca, Red Knife, and Mole on the Face are as we last saw them.

>   RED KNIFE
>   (To Rebecca; caustic)
>   "Where's the trader?"

Rebecca doesn't understand; shakes her head. Red Knife takes a step toward her.

>   RED KNIFE
>   (Continuing; impatient)
>   Barkley!

>   REBECCA
>   He... He come back soon.

The Indian doesn't really understand her. They stare at each other for a long moment. Then, Red Knife walks further into the room; looks around.

>   RED KNIFE
>   (To Rebecca)
>   "Whiskey!"

Rebecca shakes her head, not understanding.

> MOLE ON THE FACE
> (Nods; grins)
> "Whiskey!"

He points toward the counter where Barkley kept his whiskey jugs.

Rebecca understands, but feigns ignorance. She shakes her head; shrugs.

EXT. TRADING POST YARD. DAY.

The hard rain persists. In the lean-to, Iron Bear and Owl Eyes continue to inspect the horses and oxen. Obviously, they're intending to take the lot with them. Their backs are turned and they are, thus, unaware of Hawk, hobbling from the schooner wagon over to the side of the trading post building.

Hawk reaches the side of the building; presses himself against it. He is finding it difficult to maneuver about, holding both the crutch and the Henry. He moves over to the side of the porch, and listens.

From inside the building:

> RED KNIFE (O.S.)
> "Whiskey!"

In the lean-to, the two Pawnee braves complete their inspection; start back toward the front of the building.

INT. TRADING POST. DAY.

Rebecca, Red Knife and Mole on the Face are as we last saw them. Red Knife leers at the woman; starts moving toward her.

Mole on the Face crosses to the counter; starts to move behind it.

Suddenly, Rebecca produces the revolver from under the counter; grasps it with both hands.

                    REBECCA
            You hold it right there!

The Indians are startled; freeze in place.

Her hands trembling, Rebecca pulls back the hammer, cocking the weapon. She moves it back and forth between the two men, keeping them both covered.

Red Knife pulls a Bowie knife from his belt. He smiles; starts to chuckle.

                    RED KNIFE
                (To Mole on the Face)
            "Woman too frightened to fire
            gun."

Mole on the Face nods; joins his laughter. He takes another step toward Rebecca, as does Red Knife.

EXT. TRADING POST YARD. DAY.

Hawk hobbles around the porch, trying to get a better view of what is happening inside the building.

Iron Bear and Owl Eyes suddenly round the corner of the building; spot Hawk.

                    IRON BEAR
                    (To Owl Eyes)
            "Cheyenne!"

The Pawnee raise their muskets.

Hawk sees Iron Bear and Owl Eyes; spins around, grasping the Henry. The crutch falls out from under his arm, and he tumbles backward into the mud...just as the two Pawnee FIRE their muskets.

The musket balls slam into the porch where Hawk had been standing a moment before.

On the ground, Hawk recovers quickly. He FIRES the Henry, hitting Owl Eyes square in the chest. The young brave falls dead. Startled, Iron Bear dashes off behind the building.

INT. TRADING POST. DAY.

Red Knife and Mole on the Face react to the shots.

An unnerved Rebecca accidentally pulls the trigger; FIRES her revolver.

The slug smashes into a post, inches from Red Knife's head. The Pawnee ducks.

EXT. TRADING POST YARD. DAY.

Hawk grabs the crutch; struggles to his feet. Sloshing through the mud, he heads toward the front of the porch.

INT. TRADING POST. DAY.

Musket ready, Mole on the Face rushes toward the front door. Rebecca FIRES wild after him. The bullet hits him in the butt. He screams in pain; limps toward the door. Red Knife, in a crouching position, is right behind him.

EXT. TRADING POST YARD. DAY.

Hawk is halfway up the porch steps when Mole on the Face appears in the doorway. The two men glower at each other for a moment, then despite his pain, the Pawnee raises his musket to fire at the Cheyenne.

Hawk is quicker with the Henry. He FIRES at the Pawnee, hitting him in the forehead. Mole on the Face tumbles over the porch, falling face down into the mud.

Hawk turns to face the doorway, but before he can, Red Knife leaps out at him, striking Hawk on the shoulder with the butt of his musket. Hawk drops the Henry and his crutch. He reaches out and grabs Red Knife's shirt. Tangled together, the two men tumble down the stairs into the mud.

INT. TRADING POST. DAY.

Rebecca rushes to the front door.

Behind her, the rear door opens. Iron Bear, musket ready, enters quietly.

EXT. TRADING POST YARD. DAY.

Hawk and Red Knife scuffle in the mud. Because of his splinted leg, the Cheyenne appears to be getting the worst of it.

Red Knife produces his Bowie knife; raises it to plunge into Hawk's chest. Hawk grabs his arm, and they continue to struggle.

Rebecca, holding the revolver, watches from the doorway. She would like to shoot the Pawnee, but there is no clear shot.

Inside the trading post, Iron Bear steals toward her.

With his good leg, Hawk knees Red Knife in the groin. The Pawnee drops the knife into the mud. With another knee in the groin, Red Knife falls off Hawk.

INT. TRADING POST. DAY.

Iron Bear is halfway across the room, moving quietly, quickly toward Rebecca.

Rebecca becomes aware of movement behind her. She turns; spots the Pawnee. She gasps.

Iron Bear hesitates momentarily, then leaps at the woman.

Rebecca FIRES the revolver.

Iron Bear is hit in the gut, but he keeps coming.

She FIRES again.

The Indian collapses at her feet; grasps her skirt with one hand, as he reaches out at her with his other.

Rebecca screams. Then, slowly, Iron Bear releases his grip on her; lies still.

EXT. TRADING POST YARD. DAY.

Red Knife scrambles to his feet; prepares to leap onto the still prone Hawk. A SHOT. He stops; looks up toward the porch, and sees:

Rebecca stands on the porch, utilizing both hands to aim her revolver straight at him. They stare at each other for a long moment.

Realizing he has been beaten, the Pawnee raises his hands in a gesture of capitulation; starts to back away.

With considerable difficulty, Hawk struggles to get up.

                    HAWK
            (Shouts to Rebecca)
    Shoot him!

                  REBECCA
  What!?!

                    HAWK
          Shoot him!

                    REBECCA
                (Hesitates)
          But... He....

Red Knife suddenly bolts; heads for his pony.

Hawk struggles to reach the Henry, but it's too far away.

Red Knife mounts his pony; gallops out of the yard.

Rebecca watches the Pawnee brave depart; hurries down the steps to aid Hawk.

                    HAWK
                (Angry)
          Why you not shoot him!?!

                    REBECCA
          He... He surrendered.

                    HAWK
          He Pawnee! My enemy! Your enemy!

                    REBECCA
          I don't care what he is. I can't
          shoot a man who's surrendered.

Hawk allows her to help him to his feet. He snatches the crutch from her; gets his footing.

                    REBECCA
                (Continuing)
          Besides, the gun was empty.

> HAWK
> Come Spring, he be back with
> more braves.... You lucky if
> he kill you.

He hobbles up the stairs. Rebecca follows, carrying the Henry. They enter the building.

INT. TRADING POST. DAY.

Rebecca follows Hawk into the room. She gets two towels; tosses him one. They wipe the water from their faces. Silence for several moments, as they avoid each other's eyes.

> REBECCA
> You want coffee?

Hawk grunts in the affirmative; sits on a bench in the store. He watches Rebecca, as she goes to the stove; begins to pour two cups. She carries a cup over to Hawk; hands it to him.

> HAWK
> (With difficulty)
> Mrs. Carver... Thank you.

Their eyes meet. She knows how hard it was for him to say those words.

> REBECCA
> (Beat)
> You're welcome, Mr. Hawk.

A quick, awkward smile, and she returns to the stove.

FADE OUT.

FADE IN:

EXT. TRADING POST YARD. DAY.

The mountains in the distance are covered with snow. The air is nippy; the ground hard.

Rebecca, very pregnant, sits on the porch in the rocking chair, wrapped in her buffalo robe, watching Hawk, as he rides a horse back and forth around the yard. Although there is a pleasant expression on her face, she does not appear happy.

Hawk's leg is no longer in a splint. After a fast gallop across the expanse, he reins the animal; trots it over to the porch. He dismounts and, exhibiting only a minor limp, quickly climbs the stairs to the porch.

                    HAWK
          Leg feel better.

                    REBECCA
               (Forced smile)
          That's good.... Guess you'll
          be leavin' soon?

                    HAWK
               (Nods)
          Must return to my people.
               (Beat)
          I hitch wagon. You come, too.

                    REBECCA
          I ain't goin' no place.

                    HAWK
               (Gently)
          Mrs. Carver... baby come soon.
          Better if you with my people.

                    REBECCA
          I don't know your people....
                (False bravado)
          I... I'm stayin' right here....
          I won't be the first woman to
          deliver her own baby.

                     HAWK
          White wagons no come 'til Spring.

                    REBECCA
          Maybe one'll come early.
                (Beat)
          You just make sure I got enough
          firewood and water before you
          go.... If that ain't too much to
          ask of a Cheyenne warrior.

                     HAWK
                (Mutters)
          You stubborn woman.

He descends the steps; starts to lead the horse back to the lean-to.

                    REBECCA
          You go back to your people.
          I'll be okay.

He mutters something nasty in Cheyenne, as he rounds the corner.

Rebecca continues to rock. She wipes a tear from her eye.

                                              DISSOLVE TO:

INT. TRADING POST. DAWN.

SOUND of hoofbeats riding away.

Rebecca is asleep in the bed, wearing a nightdress. Her eyes open.

She sits up; looks around the room, and sees:

A large stack of firewood is next to the stove.

Rebecca wraps a blanket around her shoulders; hurries to the front door and opens it.

EXT. TRADING POST YARD. DAWN.

Standing on the porch, huddled in the blanket, Rebecca watches the distant figure of Hawk on horseback, as he disappears over a rise.

> REBECCA
> (To herself)
> Damn Indian!

She remains there for a long moment.

INT. TRADING POST. DAWN.

Rebecca comes back inside. As she walks back toward the bed, she notices the Henry on the counter. She picks up the rifle; looks at it.

> REBECCA
> (To herself)
> Girl, you're gonna be just fine.

She begins to weep.

DISSOLVE TO:

INT. LEAN-TO. DAY.

A cold wind is blowing, as Rebecca, wrapped in her buffalo robe, uses a pitchfork to feed cut grass to the horses and oxen cut grass. She makes sure that there is an over abundance of food available to them.

DISSOLVE TO:

INT. TRADING POST. DAY.

Rebecca sweeps the trading post floor with Barkley's mangled broom. She stops; goes to the stove and throws in some pieces of wood. She stays by the stove, absorbing the heat.

                                                DISSOLVE TO:

INT. TRADING POST. NIGHT.

Rebecca sits alone at the table, eating a simple meal. She listens to the SOUND of the harsh wind outside.

                                                DISSOLVE TO:

INT. TRADING POST. NIGHT.

Wearing a nightdress, Rebecca gets into the bed. She puts the revolver on the floor next to an oil lamp. Slowly, she turns down the lamp.

She lies back; listens to the SOUND of the wind.

                                                DISSOLVE TO:

EXT. TRADING POST YARD. DAY.

Rebecca, wrapped in her buffalo robe, removes a box of belongings from the schooner wagon; carries it into the trading post. CAMERA TRACKS.

                                                DISSOLVE TO:

INT. TRADING POST. DAY.

Rebecca removes some of her personal belongings from the box; places them on the table near the bed. There is a tintype wedding photo of her and Matthew, a chipped ceramic figure of a little girl, a string of cheap beads, and some hair ribbons. We know these items are special to her from the caring way that she handles them.

Her attention is diverted by something lying in the darkened corner of the room. She retrieves it to discover that it is a piece of Hawk's bloodied, discarded clothing, which she'd cut from him while tending his wounds. Her first instinct is to toss the material into the stove, but she hesitates; rubs her hand gently over it.

>   DISSOLVE TO:

EXT. RIVER BANK. DAY.

The trading post is in the near background. The sun is shining, but the air is cold.

CAMERA TRACKS, as Rebecca, the buffalo robe around her shoulders, strolls along the riverbank. She stops; stares into the water, and sees:

A fish swims by her.

>   REBECCA
>   (To fish)
>   Hello, there.

The fish darts off.

>   REBECCA
>   (Continuing)
>   That's not very sociable.
>   (Beat)
>   Can't blame you much. Guess you know
>   I'm gonna have to learn to catch you some day.

She starts back up the rise toward the trading post.

EXT. TRADING POST YARD. DAY.

Returning from the river bank, she takes a detour over to the mass grave. She stands looking down at the simple wooden marker.

>   REBECCA
>   (To grave)
>   Got myself into a real pickle,
>   Matthew.... And, it's all
>   your fault.
>   (Beat)
>   No, it's my fault.... But, I
>   shouldn't've listened to you.
>   (Beat)
>   I should've gone with Hawk....
>   He'd've looked out for me....
>   Wouldn't've let nothin' bad happen.
>   (Beat)
>   But, you got me so suspicious of
>   every darn Indian that ever walked
>   the face of this Earth....
>   (Beat)
>   Hawk's a good man, Matthew.... He
>   may be a pain in the butt sometimes....
>   (Rubs her belly)
>   I'm gonna try to give you a good,
>   healthy baby, Matthew.... I think I
>   know what to do... but it sure would've
>   been nice to have some help.... You
>   might put a good word in with the Lord...
>   if that's where you are.

She starts to walk off then, as an afterthought:

                    REBECCA
                  (Continuing)
        Amen.
She walks back toward the porch.

                                        DISSOLVE TO:

EXT. TRADING POST YARD. AFTERNOON.

Rebecca exits the privy; starts walking toward the back door of the building, her hands on her belly. Moving is difficult for her now, since the baby has dropped.

She enters the building.

                                        CUT TO:

INT. TRADING POST. AFTERNOON.

Rebecca, wearing a nightdress, sits in the rocking chair, trying to accomplish some sewing. She is experiencing some physical discomfort, the first signs of labor. Suddenly, she moves her sewing; looks down at her lap. The front of her nightdress is wet.

                    REBECCA
        Damn!

She puts her sewing aside; pushes herself to her feet. Trying to put aside her innate fear, she slowly walks over to the bed. The box from the schooner wagon is next to it, made into a makeshift cradle. The box has a blanket inside of it, plus string and a sharp, clean knife on top of that.

Rebecca lowers herself down onto the bed.

                    REBECCA
                  (To her belly)
        Hope you're not gonna give me
        as much trouble as yer daddy did.

She lies back... grimaces from pain... and begins to wait.

DISSOLVE TO:

INT. TRADING POST. DUSK.

Rebecca lies on the bed, bathed in sweat, as she continues to experience the pains of labor. She is not having an easy time.

>   REBECCA
> (Moaning; rubbing her belly)
> Come on out, child. What're
> you waitin' for? A conscription
> notice?
> (Beat; shouts)
> Matthew.... In case you're somewhere
> up there watchin' over me, you'd better
> do somethin' damn quick!

As she continues to moan, CAMERA PANS to the only light in the room, a nearby oil lamp. Suddenly:

>   REBECCA (O.S.)
> (Continuing; screams)
> God! Somebody! Help me! Please!

FADE OUT.

SOUND of approaching hoofbeats.

FADE IN:

INT. TRADING POST. NIGHT.

Rebecca lies on the bed, her pale face covered with perspiration. Her eyes open, and from her P.O.V., we see:

CROW WOMAN, 60, stands over her bed; speaking some

monotone words to her in Cheyenne. The Indian's sun-bronzed, withered face bears no expression, but there is a deep sadness behind her eyes. She wears a buffalo robe over a buckskin dress.

Rebecca is more bewildered than frightened at this seemingly surreal figure next to her. Besides, the pain is the only thing that's on her mind just now.

Crow Woman begins to tug at Rebecca's arm.

> CROW WOMAN
> "Sit up! Sit up!"

Rebecca, too weak to resist, allows the Indian to pull her up into a sitting position. She cries out in pain.

> CROW WOMAN
> (Continuing)
> "Squat! Squat!"

Rebecca doesn't move.

Crow Woman turns to someone OS.

> CROW WOMAN
> (Continuing)
> "Tell her to squat."

> HAWK (O.S.)
> (Gently)
> Mrs. Carver... Squat!

Rebecca lifts her head; looks across the room, and sees:

Hawk, a concerned expression on his face, stands by the stove. Behind him, there are apparently other Indians in the room, talking amongst themselves in Cheyenne, but, just now, they are nothing but a blur to Rebecca.

                    HAWK
          Crow Woman has brought many
          children. She will help you.

Rebecca smiles weakly; nods.

                    HAWK
               (Gestures)
          Squat.

With the help of Crow Woman, Rebecca lowers herself into a squatting position; leans her back against the side of the bed for support. The old Indian woman grasps her hands; nods approval, but doesn't smile.

Hawk leaves the room, moving out into the store area to join his two other companions. They are TALL ELK, 27, a pragmatic warrior with a stately bearing, and RUNNING WOLF, 14, an unassuming youth, aspiring to be a warrior like Hawk. Both men are dressed for the cold weather.

The SOUNDS of Rebecca's pain and Crow Woman's words to her in the Cheyenne tongue remain in the background, as Hawk begins to pace the floor.

                   TALL ELK
               (Matter-of-fact)
          "Soars Like a Hawk behaves like
          the child is his own."

Hawk does not appreciate the remark; scowls at his companion, then tromps to the front door and exits outside.

                                        CUT TO:

EXT. TRADING POST YARD. NIGHT.

Four Cheyenne Warriors are camped around a fire built in the center of the trading post yard. One of them is named YELLOW

MOCCASIN, 30, however we are most aware of CRAZY BUFFALO, 24, tall and muscular; as sullen a man as his late brother, Spotted Face. Sitting close to the flames, Crazy Buffalo ignores the good natured Cheyenne banter of his companions. His skulking eyes are trained on:

Hawk, as he paces the porch. Tall Elk comes out of the building; watches Hawk.

                    TALL ELK
                (Beat)
            "Her man is dead. If you want
            her... take her."

Hawk stops pacing; moves to face Tall Elk.

                    HAWK
                (Angry)
            "I owe this woman a great debt."

                    TALL ELK
            "There are those who would take
            her captive.... Perhaps take her scalp."

He throws a quick glance in Crazy Buffalo's direction.

                    HAWK
                (With disdain)
            "I do not not worry about Crazy
            Buffalo."

                    TALL ELK
            "He blames the woman for his
            brother's murder."

                    HAWK
          "If he misses the buffalo with his arrow... he
          blames the buffalo for moving. That is why
          he is called Crazy Buffalo"
                    (Beat)
          "The woman saved my life."

                    TALL ELK
                    (Beat)
          "She is alone.... If you do
          not claim her, another will."

                    HAWK
                    (Beat)
          "You, Tall Elk?"

                    TALL ELK
                    (Shakes head)
          "Others, my brother."

He and Tall Elk stare at each other for a long time.

                                        CUT TO:

INT. TRADING POST. NIGHT.

The SOUNDS of Rebecca's pain and Crow Woman's words to her in the Cheyenne tongue continue in the background, as Running Wolf sits in a chair, feigning sleep, but actually keeping one curious eye on the activities in the back part of the room.

CLOSE SHOT

Rebecca, moaning in pain; eyes wide, her face perspiring, as she waits for the baby to come.

CLOSE SHOT

Crow Woman, eyes front, staring deep into Rebecca's eyes.

Speaking... almost chanting to her in Cheyenne.

CLOSE SHOT

Rebecca's moans suddenly cease. She looks directly at Crow Woman.

CUT TO:

EXT. TRADING POST YARD. NIGHT.

Hawk and Tall Elk are on the porch.

Inside, Rebecca SCREAMS, then:

The SOUND of a baby crying.

The Cheyenne Braves around the fire react positively to the infant's cry... except for Crazy Buffalo, who continues to scowl.

Hawk attempts to hide his smile, as he enters the trading post.

INT. TRADING POST. NIGHT.

Rebecca lies back on the bed, holding the newborn infant, wrapped in a blanket.

Crow Woman is next to the bed; Running Wolf by the stove. As Hawk approaches the bed:

                    CROW WOMAN
                      (To Hawk)
            "It is a male child."

Rebecca looks up from her baby; smiles at Hawk.

                    REBECCA
       Gonna call 'im after his daddy...
       Matthew.... Matthew Carver, Jr.

                    HAWK
            It is a good name.

                    REBECCA
                (Beat)
            Thank you, Mr. Hawk.

They continue to stare at each other.

                                        FADE OUT.

FADE IN:

EXT. TRADING POST YARD. DAY.

The sun is shining. It is a warm winter day. Running Wolf is at the lean-to, tending to the horses and oxen.

                    HAWK (O.S.)
            Running Wolf is a honorable young
            brave....

Crow Woman sits on the porch, holding the baby. In the yard in front of her, the Cheyenne warriors are tending to their weapons, cleaning up their encampment.

                    HAWK (O.S.)
                (Continuing)
            He and Crow Woman will stay with
            you and the child until the wagon
            train comes.

EXT. RIVER BANK. DAY.

CAMERA TRACKS, as Hawk and Rebecca stroll along the bank. She wears a shawl around her shoulders. There is an awkwardness in their conversation, of feelings unspoken.

                    REBECCA
What about you?

                    HAWK
My brothers and I must find the buffalo herd.
I will try to return before you go.

                    REBECCA
          (Beat)
I might not go.

                    HAWK
Not go!?!

                    REBECCA
I been thinkin'.... What do I got
to go to?... No family back east....
Don't know a soul out west....

                    HAWK
Mrs. Carver is getting not too smart, again.

                    REBECCA
My husband is buried here. My
son was born here. Maybe this
here place is where I belong.

                    HAWK
This land is for Cheyenne...
not lone white woman.

                    REBECCA
How hard can it be to run a
trading post? Mr. Barkley did it
without much help.... You trade
store goods to the Indians for buffalo
hides, and you trade the hides to get
the store goods.

She beams a satisfied smile at him.

                    HAWK
            That foolish idea!
                (At a loss)
            Mrs. Carver must have friends in east....

                    REBECCA
                (Beat)
            Mr. Hawk, you're the only friend I got.

Her admission startles Hawk. Indeed, it even surprises her. Not knowing how to respond to her, he leaves the river bank; heads up the rise toward the trading post yard.

EXT. TRADING POST YARD. DAY.

Hawk shouts some orders in Cheyenne to his fellow warriors, apparently telling them to mount up. He mounts his own horse; swiftly rides out of the yard, past Crazy Buffalo, who is stowing the bow he had been mending. Hawk is quickly out of sight.

The sullen Crazy Buffalo watches Hawk depart; then, mounting his animal, he glances over at Rebecca, who observes the departing band from the river bank.

                    TALL ELK (O.S.)
        "We ride!"

Tall Elk, on his mount, scowls at Crazy Buffalo; motions him to follow. The Indians ride out of the yard, taking with them a string of pack horses.

                                        CUT TO:

EXT. THE PRAIRIE. DAY.

Hawk rides his horse up to the top of a rise; reins it to a halt. He dismounts; squats on the ground, as he ponders the situation.

A few moments later, the band of Cheyenne, led by Tall Elk and Crazy Buffalo, appear behind him; ride to where he has stopped.

                    CRAZY BUFFALO
            "Does Soars Like a Hawk seek the
            buffalo or the white woman?"

                    HAWK
            "My brother has a loose tongue."

                    CRAZY BUFFALO
            "My brother, Spotted Face, is with
            his ancestors.

Hawk stands to confront Crazy Buffalo.

                    HAWK
            "You have been told. The white woman
            was not responsible."

                    CRAZY BUFFALO
            "She is bad medicine."

Behind him, Yellow Moccasin and the other Cheyenne braves nod in agreement.

                    TALL ELK
                (Placating)
            "The woman and her child will leave soon...
            when the white man's wagons come. Until
            then, she must be tolerated...
                (Indicates Hawk)
            ...for saving our brother's life."

More murmurings from the Cheyenne braves, agreeing now with Tall Elk.

                    CRAZY BUFFALO
                (Beat)
            "But, will the woman leave with the
            white man's wagons?"

Tall Elk looks to Hawk for an answer. Hawk does not have one. He averts his eyes; turns and points toward the horizon.

> HAWK
> "We ride north to seek the buffalo."

More mutterings among the Cheyenne, as Hawk mounts his horse; rides away. The braves follow.

> CUT TO:

EXT. TRADING POST YARD. DAY.

CAMERA TRACKS Rebecca, as she walks from the river bank up to the trading post building. She mounts the porch; approaches Crow Woman, who holds the sleeping baby. The poker faced Indian woman gets up; dutifully hands the infant over to Rebecca.

> REBECCA
> Thank you.

The Indian does not acknowledge her. Rebecca sits in the chair; watches Crow Woman, as she walks down toward the river bank.

> CUT TO:

INT. TRADING POST. NIGHT.

Rebecca is at the table, eating her supper with knife and fork. Running Wolf sits opposite her, eating with his fingers. He keeps his eyes on his plate, apparently uncomfortable being so close to the white woman.

In the back of the room, next to the sleeping baby in the makeshift cradle, Crow Woman sits, back turned, eating from a plate with her fingers.

                    REBECCA
               (Trying to make
               conversation)
          You do good work, Running
          Wolf. I sure do appreciate your help.

Running Wolf grunts acknowledgement; does not look at her.

                    REBECCA
               (Continuing; beat)
          I know you'd rather be out
          lookin' for buffalo with....

                    RUNNING WOLF
          Soars Like a Hawk tell Running Wolf
          to stay... help Mrs. Carver. Running
          Wolf obey.

He stuffs another piece of food into his mouth. Rebecca also takes a bite, then, after a glance at Crow Woman:

                    REBECCA
               (Whisper)
          Why doesn't Crow Woman sit
          with us?

                    RUNNING WOLF
          Not know. Ask Crow Woman.

                    REBECCA
          I don't think she likes me.

                    RUNNING WOLF
          She like.

                    REBECCA
          She never smiles at me.

                    RUNNING WOLF
          She no smile at nobody. That no
          mean she no like.

Rebecca looks over at Crow Woman, who continues to eat, back turned, then looks back at Running Wolf, who keeps his eyes on his food.

                    REBECCA
               (Beat)
          She's Hawk's mother?

Running Wolf looks at her briefly, nods. He returns to his eating.

                                        CUT TO:

EXT. THE PRAIRIE. NIGHT.

The night is dark; temperature warming. The Cheyenne warriors are eating, chatting amiably around a campfire. Hawk, reflective, sits apart from them.

                                        CUT TO:

INT. TRADING POST. NIGHT.

Rebecca, dressed for and lying on the bed, finishes nursing the baby; puts him into the makeshift cradle. Her breast remains exposed.

Across the room in the store area, Crow Woman and Running Wolf lay on the floor in makeshift beds. Exhibiting the curiosity expected from any young man his age, Running Wolf raises his head slightly to gaze upon Rebecca's nudity.

Suddenly, without raising her head, Crow Woman slaps the youth on the hand, mutters a few scolding words in Cheyenne.

Getting the message, an embarrassed Running Wolf turns away from Rebecca; puts his head down.

Unaware of Running Wolf's peeping, Rebecca covers herself; looks affectionately at her sleeping infant.

She lies back onto the bed; notices the piece of Hawk's bloodied, discarded clothing on the table next to her. She picks it up; holds it to her.

CUT TO:

EXT. THE PRAIRIE. DAY.

It is a warm day. Spring is near.

CAMERA TRACKS Hawk, Tall Elk, Crazy Buffalo, Yellow Moccasin and the other Cheyenne, as they ride along a stream, then up to the top of a rise, where they rein their horses.

On the plain below them, there is no sign of the buffalo herd.

> HAWK
> "The herd is cunning.... It would be wise if we rode in different directions."

> TALL ELK
> (Nods)
> "We would cover more ground."

The other warriors nod agreement.

> HAWK
> "We will rendezvous at the trading post in three days."

Crazy Buffalo appears suspicious of Hawk's suggestion, but he remains silent.

> TALL ELK
> (Nods)
> "Three days."

Hawk rides off by himself. The other Cheyenne break off either in pairs or solo, fanning out in different directions.

> CUT TO:

EXT. TRADING POST YARD. DAWN.

The sun is just coming up. Horses are back in the corral.

Nobody appears to be about on this warm morning, as Rebecca emerges from the building, carrying soap and a towel. CAMERA TRACKS her, as she heads for the river bank.

Running Wolf steps out of the lean-to, where he has been tending to the oxen. Unknown to her, he observes Rebecca, as she descends to the river bank. A moment later, he steals after her.

CAMERA TRACKS Running Wolf, as he moves toward the river bank. As he draws close, he drops to a crouching position; creeps to the edge of the slope overlooking the water.

Below him, Rebecca, naked, stands in the cool water up to her knees. She faces in his direction, as she bathes herself.

Running Wolf is fascinated by the forbidden sight.

Rebecca, continues to wash; dip herself into the river, still unaware that she is being watched.

Still crouching, Running Wolf moves closer to the edge for a better view.

> HAWK (O.S.)
> "Has my little brother seen
> enough?"

Startled, Running Wolf spins around and sees:

Hawk stands over him, looking both disappointed and amused.

Running Wolf loses his balance; tumbles down the slope and into the water next to Rebecca.

Even more startled, Rebecca screams. She covers her breasts with her hands; submerges herself into the river to hide her nakedness.

As an embarrassed Running Wolf swims; makes his way out of the river, a blushing Rebecca looks up and sees:

Hawk stands on top of the slope, looking down at her.

> HAWK
> (Calls; amused)
> Good morning, Mrs. Carver.

Rebecca stays in the water; continues to blush. Hawk waves; walks out of sight, as Running Wolf scrambles up the embankment after him.

> CUT TO:

EXT. TRADING POST YARD. DAWN.

Rebecca, fully clothed, ascends from the riverbank. Reaching the top of the slope, she tromps toward the trading post.

> HAWK (O.S.)
> Mrs. Carver....

Rebecca spins and sees:

Hawk walks toward her from the corral. He leads his own horse and one other, which is saddled.

REBECCA
            (Embarrassed; irate)
        What're you doin' here, Mr. Hawk?

                    HAWK
        Running Wolf young. He never see
        white woman before.... He hide...
        feel great shame.

                    REBECCA
            (Still irate)
        What about you?

                    HAWK
            (A mischievous glint)
        I never see white woman either.

Rebecca can't help but smile at the Indian's stoic admission. He walks over to her.

                    HAWK
            (Beat)
        Come. Ride with me.
        We must talk.

Rebecca nods. He helps her onto the horse, then after quickly mounting himself, they ride out of the yard.

As they disappear over the horizon, Crow Woman appears in the doorway of the trading post; watches them.

                            CUT TO:

EXT. THE PRAIRIE. MORNING

A HELICOPTER SHOT initially tracks Rebecca and Hawk, as they ride through the seemingly endless plain. Reaching the top of a hill, they rein their horses to a stop.

Hawk dismounts; surveys the openness before them. Rebecca also dismounts; joins him.

> HAWK
> This land.... It all belong to
> Cheyenne. My father... my uncle....
> They die defending it from Pawnee...
> from Kiowa.... My brothers.... They
> die defending it from the white man....
> And, my mother no longer smiles.

> REBECCA
> I know that Crow Woman is your
> mother.

> HAWK
> (Nods; beat)
> I have thought on this, Mrs. Carver.
> (Beat)
> I like you.... I have "feelings" for you....

> REBECCA
> (Surprised)
> Mr. Hawk!

> HAWK
> But, to be your "friend" would
> be to betray my people.

> REBECCA
> Mr. Barkley was your friend.

> HAWK
> Barkley married my cousin. He
> became one of our people.
> (Beat)
> Do you wish to marry a Cheyenne,
> and live as a Cheyenne woman?

REBECCA
No.

HAWK
And, I do not wish to live as a white man.

REBECCA
(Beat)
Who said anything 'bout getting married?... Couldn't you just come and visit?

HAWK
(Beat)
I come visit... until Mrs. Carver leave.

REBECCA
I told you. I ain't leavin'.

HAWK
(Mutters, annoyed)
Foolish... stubborn woman....

REBECCA
You already called me that. Sayin' it again don't make it any more so.

HAWK
When the fighting between your people and my people begin... I will stand with the Cheyenne. I will not help you.

REBECCA
What about the mountain lion and the grizzly bear? Thought you were goin' to avoid fightin'?

                    HAWK
          I am but one voice. I do not yet sit
          in tribal Council.

                    REBECCA
          Well, talk to 'em. They'll listen.

Hawk cannot help but be amused by her naivete. He tries to avoid smiling; almost succeeds.

                    REBECCA
               (Continuing; irked)
          What's so funny?

                    HAWK
          Mrs. Carver may be foolish... stubborn.
          She also very... confusing.

                    REBECCA
               (Chuckles)
          What's wrong with that? I use to
          confuse Matthew all the time.

                    HAWK
               (Nods)
          Maybe safer... not confused.

He smiles at her. She grins in return. The stare at each other with affection for a long moment, then:

                    HAWK
               (Continuing)
          It will not work, Mrs. Carver.

                    REBECCA
          Can't we try?... Just bein' friends.

                              HAWK
                  (Beat)
            We try.

Fighting the temptation to touch, they continue to look at each other.

                                        CUT TO:

EXT. THE PRAIRIE. DAY.

CAMERA TRACKS Rebecca and Hawk, as they ride back toward the trading post.

                                        CUT TO:

EXT. TRADING POST YARD. DAY.

Hawk and Rebecca ride into the yard. They rein their horses to an abrupt halt when they see:

Crazy Buffalo, Tall Elk, Yellow Moccasin and the other Cheyenne braves stand in the center of the yard, waiting for them. There are angry expressions on their faces.

Running Wolf watches from the corral. Crow Woman, holding the baby, stands on the porch.

Hawk trots his horse over to the braves.

                              HAWK
                        (Greeting them;
                         wary)
                  "My brothers...."

                         CRAZY BUFFALO
                        (With hatred)
                  "Soars Like a Hawk has betrayed
                  the Cheyenne."

The remark is like a slap in the face to Hawk. He leaps off his horse; stands face-to-face with Crazy Buffalo.

Rebecca tenses at the confrontation.

> HAWK
> "Crazy Buffalo speaks dangerous words."

> CRAZY BUFFALO
> "Instead of seeking out the buffalo, you have betrayed us for a white harlot."

Hawk's face reddens. Without thinking, he smashes Crazy Buffalo in the face with his fist.

Crazy Buffalo staggers a step back, but does not fall. He draws his Bowie knife from it's sheath; leaps at Hawk.

> CRAZY BUFFALO
> (Shouts)
> "Traitor!"

Hawk grabs Crazy Buffalo, deflecting the knife. The two men go sprawling onto the ground.

Rebecca gasps; dismounts. She rushes over toward the struggling men. As they fight for control of the knife:

> REBECCA
> (Shouts to Tall Elk)
> Stop them!

Tall Elk merely scowls at her. He turns his attention back to the struggle.

Crazy Buffalo maneuvers on top of Hawk; raises the knife to plunge it downward into his chest.

Rebecca, desperately, leaps onto Crazy Buffalo's back, pulling him off of Hawk.

The Cheyenne men chuckle at the sight of Crazy Buffalo struggling on the ground with the white woman, who is beginning to tear at his hair.

Hawk gets to his feet; pulls Rebecca off of Crazy Buffalo, who scrambles to his feet.

>   HAWK
>   (Firm)
>   Mrs. Carver... <u>don't</u> <u>interfere</u>!

He pushes her to one side, turns back toward Crazy Buffalo.

Crazy Buffalo, still holding the knife, leaps at Hawk. With one hand, Hawk deflects Crazy Buffalo's knife, and with the other the lands a haymaker onto the Indian's jaw.

Crazy Buffalo staggers backward. Hawk draws his own Bowie knife; advances toward his adversary.

>   REBECCA
>   (Mutters; to herself)
>   Think I'm gonna let you get
>   killed?... Leave me out here all
>   alone?

Rebecca rushes past the fighting men; heads for the trading post building. She mounts the stairs; pushes past Crow Woman, who now stares at her with resentment, and enters the building. Hawk and Crazy Buffalo square-off, begin circling against each other.

Yellow Moccasin takes a step forward, planning to break up the confrontation. Tall Elk grabs his arm; stops him.

>   TALL ELK
> "Now or later, they must fight
> this out."

Crazy Buffalo lunges at Hawk, who jumps aside. They continue to circle.

Rebecca rushes out of the house. She carries the Henry; stands on the porch next to Crow Woman, who continues to hold the baby.

>   REBECCA
>   (Shouts)
> Stop!

The men ignore her. Rebecca aims the rifle at them.

>   REBECCA
>   (Continuing;
>   mutters)
> Darn it! This time, I will shoot.

The expressionless Crow Woman bumps Rebecca with her hip. Rebecca momentarily loses her balance. The Henry accidently DISCHARGES.

The wild shot strikes Yellow Moccasin in the head, knocking him down.

Hawk and Crazy Buffalo stop circling.

The other Indians turn their attention toward Rebecca.

Rebecca has recovered her footing. Still holding the Henry, she moves down the steps, keeping one eye on Crow Woman, who does not move, and the rifle loosely trained on the Cheyenne.

> REBECCA
> (Frightened)
> Is he dead?
> (To Hawk)
> It was an accident.

Hawk doesn't answer. He, like the others, stands frozen, stunned by the turn of events.

Tall Elk kneels next to the unconscious Yellow Moccasin.

Crazy Buffalo doesn't wait to hear from Tall Elk. He stalks toward Rebecca, his Bowie knife poised for the kill.

> CRAZY BUFFALO
> (Shouts)
> "Murderer!"

Hawk springs at Crazy Buffalo. He grabs him from the rear, locking his arm around his neck, and pulling him backwards onto the ground. With both men on their knees, Hawk presses his Bowie knife against Crazy Buffalo's throat.

> HAWK
> "You will not touch her!"

> CRAZY BUFFALO
> "You protect the enemy who
> has killed your brother?"

Tall Elk stands; moves over to Crazy Buffalo and Hawk.

> TALL ELK
> "It is only a graze. Yellow
> Moccasin will recover."

Behind him, the other braves help Yellow Moccasin to sit up.

                    HAWK
         "Then there is no murder!"

Hawk pushes Crazy Buffalo forward onto his face. He springs to his feet; joins Rebecca by the building. He takes the Henry from her; points it at the other Cheyenne.

                    HAWK
                  (Continuing)
         "Leave this place... before there
         is killing among us!"

                    TALL ELK
                  (Takes a step toward
                  him)
         "Soars Like a Hawk forgets that he is Cheyenne."

                    HAWK
                  (Snaps)
         "I do not forget!"

He indicates Crazy Buffalo, who is getting to his feet.

                    HAWK
                  (Continuing)
         "It is my brothers who forget,
         and listen to one who speaks lies"

                    TALL ELK
         "Do you choose this white woman
         over your people?"

                    HAWK
         "I will protect my friend, Mrs. Carver.
         It is for my people to choose."

Tall Elk ponders Hawk's statement. The other Cheyenne confer quietly among themselves.

Rebecca remains behind Hawk. She appears confused over what has taken place.

                          HAWK
                      (Continuing)
                  "Go now!"

Tall Elk, Crazy Buffalo, Yellow Moccasin and the other Cheyenne move to their horses. As they mount:

                          HAWK
                    (Continuing; calls)
                  "The buffalo. They are to the
                  east. In the valley of the tall
                  grass."

Tall Elk, Crazy Buffalo and the other Cheyenne are surprised at Hawk's news. Indeed, they appear somewhat chagrined.

                          HAWK
                      (Continuing)
                  "Go!"

He FIRES the Henry into the air. The Cheyenne ride out of the yard.

Hawk turns to Rebecca. There is a sadness, a sense of loss in his eyes. He hands her the Henry.

                        REBECCA
                  Mr. Hawk...?

He walks away, heading toward the river bank. Rebecca does not move; watches him disappear down the slope.

After a moment, the expressionless Crow Woman descends the stairs; thrusts the baby into Rebecca's arms, then walks off toward the lean-to.

Over at the corral, Running Wolf stares at Rebecca, then turns and walks away.

Rebecca, holding back tears, hurries up the steps with her baby; enters the house.

From the direction of the river bank, we HEAR Hawk's voice as he sings a Cheyenne funeral chant.

CUT TO:

EXT. RIVER BANK. NIGHT.

The moon is full, as Rebecca makes her way down the slope to the river's edge. She spots Hawk, sitting cross-legged on the ground, staring off into the distance.

>REBECCA
>(Tentative)
>Mr. Hawk...?

>HAWK
>(Noncommittal)
>Mrs. Carver.

>REBECCA
>Got supper waitin'.

Hawk grunts an acknowledgement, but still does not look at her. She walks over to him.

>REBECCA
>(Continuing; beat)
>Can't tell you how bad I feel
>'bout what happened today.

>HAWK
>(Beat)
>Mrs. Carver must go.

                    REBECCA
                (Shakes head)
            Thought we settled that?

                    HAWK
            Trading post no longer safe.

                    REBECCA
            Who said it ever was?

                    HAWK
                (Stands)
            I will not kill my brothers.

                    REBECCA
                (Beat)
            I never wanted you to fight
            with your people... 'specially
            'bout me....

                    HAWK
            Then, you will go!

                    REBECCA
            <u>No</u>! If you want to leave, that's
            one thing. But, I'm stayin'.

She turns; makes her way back up the slope. Hawk watches her depart.

                                        CUT TO:

INT. LEAN-TO. NIGHT.

Crow Woman sits alone in the darkness. She is lost in her own thoughts.

Hawk appears at the entrance, silhouetted by the moonlight.

                    HAWK
        "My mother... I must talk to
        you."

                    CROW WOMAN
        "About the woman?"

                    HAWK
            (Nods)
        "I.... I care for her."

                    CROW WOMAN
            (Beat)
        "My son... you know what you
        must do."

Their eyes lock.

                                        CUT TO:

INT. TRADING POST. NIGHT.

A despondent Rebecca sits alone at the table, eating her supper. The baby sleeps in the nearby makeshift cradle.

SOUNDS of footsteps on the porch outside.

Rebecca watches the entrance with anticipation.

Suddenly the door slams open. Hawk enters, followed by Running Wolf and Crow Woman.

Crow Woman walks over; picks up the baby. Running Wolf moves behind the counter; grabs a box of food.

                    REBECCA
            (Startled)
        What... What's goin' on!?!

                    HAWK
          We go now!

                    REBECCA
          Go where!?!

Running Wolf heads for the door. Crow Woman, carrying the baby, starts after him.

                    REBECCA
                  (Continuing)
          Give me my baby!

Rebecca grabs hold of Crow Woman's arm. Hawk moves forward, restrains Rebecca.

                    REBECCA
                  (Continuing; screams)
          Stop this!!

Crow Woman exits with the infant, as Rebecca struggles with Hawk. The Cheyenne takes a strip of rawhide from his belt, begins to tie her hands behind her back.

                    REBECCA
                  (Continuing; suddenly
                   frightened)
          What...!?! Are you takin' me captive!?!

                    HAWK
          Mrs. Carver will go!

Running Wolf returns for more supplies.

                    REBECCA
                  (Incensed)
          I thought you were my friend!...
          Dirty stinkin' Indian!!
She begins to kick at him with little success.

> HAWK
> Mrs. Carver talk too much.

With another strip of rawhide, he gags Rebecca. Then, with her still struggling, he throws her over his shoulder and carries her outside.

EXT. TRADING POST YARD. NIGHT.

Hawk emerges from the building with the bound, gagged and unceasingly kicking Rebecca over his shoulder. Her muffled protests are still loud through the rawhide. He carries her to the schooner wagon, which has been hitched to the oxen.

Crow Woman stands nearby, holding the baby.

> HAWK
> (To Crow Woman)
> "Tie her feet."

He deposits Rebecca face down onto the ground, while Crow Woman carefully puts the baby into the front of the wagon. As Hawk heads back toward the building, Crow Woman sits on Rebecca's rear end, as she ties her kicking feet together.

CUT TO:

INT. TRADING POST. NIGHT.

Hawk reenters the store, just as Running Wolf is carrying out another load of supplies.

Hawk walks slowly to the back of the building, inspecting its contents. He arrives at the bed, and sees:

The tintype wedding photo, chipped ceramic figure and Rebecca's other personal items, sitting on the table by the bed. There is also the torn, bloodied piece of his clothing.

Hawk picks up the torn cloth, examines it briefly, then tosses it aside. He scoops up the other items, grabs some of Rebecca's clothing and heads back into the store area.

Running Wolf, back in the store, is on his way out again with another box of goods. Indeed, behind the counter, almost everything of value has been removed.

Hawk puts Rebecca's clothing and personal belongings on top of Running Wolf's box; motions him push on.

As the youth exits, Hawk spots the Henry on the counter. He walks over; snaps it up. Then, his eyes fall on:

A lit oil lamp.

CUT TO:

EXT. TRADING POST YARD. NIGHT.

Bound and gagged, Rebecca leans against the wagon, facing the building. Tears of frustration are in her eyes.

Running Wolf, arms full with the box, plus Rebecca's clothing and personal items, comes out of the building. He crosses over to the schooner wagon; quickly shows the personal items to Rebecca.

> RUNNING WOLF
> (With respect)
> These important to you?

Rebecca's eyes blaze anger at seeing her personal things touched by others.

Running Wolf tosses the items into the rear of the wagon. He avoids Rebecca's stare; returns to the trading post building.

Rebecca rubs her rawhide gag against the wagon wheel in an attempt to free it from her mouth.

INT. TRADING POST. NIGHT.

Running Wolf enters, grabs a final box of trade goods. He looks over at Hawk, who watches him... waiting for him to depart.

                    HAWK
    Go!

Running Wolf exits.

Hawk crosses to the oil lamp, picks it up. He crosses back to the doorway, turns and surveys the room one last time.

A look of determination, mixed with sadness, is on his face, as he tosses the lamp hard against the wall.

The room IGNITES into FLAMES.

Hawk exits.

EXT. TRADING POST YARD. NIGHT.

Hawk crosses to the wagon.

Rebecca, the gag now off her mouth, watches horrified, as the flames consume the fragile trading post building. She begins to weep.

                  REBECCA
              (To Hawk)
  I hate you!

Hawk does not like what he has done. He avoids looking at Rebecca, as he helps Running Wolf load the store goods into the wagon.

                    REBECCA
                  (Continuing)
            I hate you!

                                          CUT TO:

EXT. THE PRAIRIE. DAY.

The prairie schooner, pulled by the oxen, moves slowly along the plain. Waning smoke from the dying conflagration is far in the distance. Hawk drives the wagon; Crow Woman sits on the seat next to him. Running Wolf follows on horseback, leading the string of ponies that were in Barkley's corral.

INT. SCHOONER WAGON. DAY.

Now untied, a melancholy Rebecca rides in the back of the wagon. She is turned away from Hawk and Crow Woman, as she nurses the baby. They ride in silence.

EXT. THE PRAIRIE. DAY.

The prairie schooner and accompanying horses continue across the plain.

                                          CUT TO:

EXT. THE PRAIRIE. NIGHT.

The travelers have stopped for the night. A campfire has been built. Hawk, Crow Woman and Running Wolf sit around the blaze, eating their evening meal. Rebecca sits off to one side, holding the sleeping baby.

Hawk puts down his plate; gets up, walks over to Rebecca and sits.

                    HAWK
        Mrs. Carver cold? Want buffalo robe?

She shakes her head; turns away from him. Then, after a moment:

                    REBECCA
                    (Resigned)
        When do we get to your camp?

                    HAWK
        No go to camp.

                    REBECCA
                    (Surprised)
        I thought you...?

                    HAWK
        Mrs. Carver thought she would be
        captive of Cheyenne? Squaw, maybe?

Rebecca remains open mouthed; doesn't answer.

                    HAWK
                    (Continuing)
        Mrs. Carver too much trouble to be
        Cheyenne captive.... We take you
        east to your own people.

Hawk stands, as Rebecca takes a few moments to let this news register, then:

                    REBECCA
                    (Bitter)
        Did you have to burn the place down?

                    HAWK
        Mrs. Carver might try to come back.

He starts to walk away from her.

                    REBECCA
              (Angry; shouts at
               his back)
          I'm gettin' sick of your funny sayin's!
                    (Beat)
          Thought you had feelin's for me.

The retort stings at Hawk. He wants to reply; decides against it. He rejoins Crow Woman and Running Wolf.

                                        CUT TO:

EXT. THE PRAIRIE. DAY.

The schooner wagon and horses move across the plain.

                                        DISSOLVE TO:

EXT. RIVER. DAY.

Moving slowly, the schooner wagon and horses traverse the river at a shallow point. Crow Woman now rides a horse. Holding her baby, Rebecca sits on the front seat of the wagon next to Hawk. She does not appear to be happy.

                                        DISSOLVE TO:

EXT. THE PRAIRIE. AFTERNOON.

The schooner wagon and horses continue on its journey east, passing through surroundings filled with rocks and high brush.

Running Wolf trots his pony up to the front of the wagon, so that he rides next to Hawk.

                    RUNNING WOLF
              (Points in the distance)
          Riders come.

                    HAWK
                (Nods)
        I see.

Somewhat anxious, Rebecca peers, squints up ahead.

Far in the distance, we SEE three horsemen approaching. It is impossible for us to tell if they are white or Indian.

                    HAWK (O.S.)
                (Continuing)
        White men.

Hawk reins the horses; jumps down onto the ground, taking the Henry with him.

                    HAWK
                (To Rebecca)
        Mrs. Carver should get in back of wagon.

                    REBECCA
                (Confused)
        You said they were white men!?!

                    HAWK
        Not know what kind of white men yet.

Understanding his caution, Rebecca obeys.

Hawk shouts something in Cheyenne to Crow Woman, who dismounts; moves up behind the wagon. Running Wolf also dismounts; ducks behind the wagon, holding his muzzle-loading rifle at the ready.

Holding onto the Henry, Hawk drops to one knee; waits for the riders to arrive.

                                        CUT TO:

EXT. THE PRAIRIE. AFTERNOON.

A few minutes later. Hawk and the others are as we last saw them.

The three riders approach: JACK ANDREWS, 27, would-be hunter, trapper and scout. A mustache across his lip, Andrews wears a buckskin shirt and striped pants issued by the Union Army. He is tall; a friendly, cautious man, who walks with a limp. He, like Hawk, has a Henry rifle, plus a Colt in his gunbelt.

With Andrews are AMOS GRUBER, 35, a bearded German immigrant of medium build; and another bearded immigrant, named JACOB, 35. Both of the Germans wear clothing native to their own country; carry Sharps rifles

As the strangers reach the wagon, Hawk stands; assumes a non-threatening stance, as he raises his hand in greeting.

The riders register surprise. Andrews moves a wary hand to the handle of his Colt. He and Hawk study each other for a moment.

                    ANDREWS
                (Wary)
What're you doin' here, Indian?

                    HAWK
                (Beat)
That for me to ask. You are on
Cheyenne land.

                    ANDREWS
                (Beat)
Name's Andrews.... I got ten wagons of
foreigners... sodbusters... 'bout three
hours behind me. Takin' 'em up to the
Oregon country.

Suddenly, Andrews whips out his Colt; levels it at Hawk. The two Germans also cover the Cheyenne with their weapons.

From behind the wagon, a hidden Running Wolf aims at Andrews with his rifle.

                      ANDREWS
                  (Continuing)
    Now, answer <u>my</u> question, Indian....
    What're you doin' here with a white
    man's wagon...?
               (Indicates Henry)
    <u>And</u>, a white man's rifle?

Hawk doesn't answer. He stands proud; unflinching.

Andrews and his companions exchange glances. Andrews pulls back the hammer on his Colt.

                    REBECCA (O.S.)
    I give it to him.

Rebecca, baby in her arms, appears behind the front seat of the wagon.

Andrews and his two companions are startled to see her. Gruber and Jacob exchange a few words in German.

                      ANDREWS
                  (Beat)
    Why would you do that, ma'm?

                      REBECCA
                  (Matter of fact)
    He an' his friends helped me
    after my husband were killed.

                      ANDREWS
  Indians?

                    REBECCA
              (Shakes head)
        Renegade whites.... Killed Mr.
        Barkley at the tradin' post, too.

                    ANDREWS
              (Surprised)
        Barkley's dead!?!

                    REBECCA
              (Nods)
        Mr. Hawk, here, was bringin' me and
        my baby back to my own people.

She eyes Hawk without warmth. His eyes reveal understanding;
appreciation toward her.

                    ANDREWS
              (Not sure he believes her)
        That was right nice of him.

Hawk's attention is attracted to something in the distance behind
Andrews.

                    REBECCA (O.S.)
              (A tinge of sarcasm)
        He's a Cheyenne warrior chief.

About fifty yards away, there is a movement on the ground, as if
somebody was slowly crawling forward.

                    ANDREWS
              (Beat)
        You don't say....
              (To Hawk)
        Warrior chief, huh?
              (Beat)
        Them dozen or so Indian bucks that been
        trailin' us the last half hour belong to you?

HAWK
              No.... Them Pawnee!

Hawk, abruptly, raises his Henry; FIRES beyond Andrews.

                   ANDREWS
                   (Startled)
              <u>Jesus</u>!

Thinking he is firing at him, Andrews FIRES at Hawk. However, Andrews' spooked horse rears, causing the shot to miss Hawk and hit the ground.

Fifty yards away, a Pawnee warrior on foot, who had been drawing a bead on Andrews with his rifle, is hit in the chest; collapses.

Caught completely off-guard, Andrews isn't sure who he should shoot at. Suddenly, an arrow zooms in from nowhere; strikes his horse in the neck with a THONK. The animal stumbles; collapses against the oxen, throwing Andrews to the ground. The oxen stand their ground.

Rebecca screams.

Another THONK, and Jacob pitches forward onto the ground, an arrow protruding from his back.

Gruber panics; FIRES wildly behind him, and hits nothing. Again, Hawk FIRES the Henry, and another Pawnee in the brush is hit.

                    HAWK
                   (Shouts)
              Mrs. Carver... <u>Get down</u>!

INT. SCHOONER WAGON. AFTERNOON.

Holding the baby, Rebecca crouches down behind the boxes of store goods. The infant starts to CRY.

EXT. THE PRAIRIE. AFTERNOON.

In the distance, a half dozen mounted Pawnee warriors, HOOPING AND HOLLERING, gallop toward the wagon. They are armed with bow and arrow, lances and a few front loading muskets. They are accompanied by three other braves on foot.

Gruber dismounts; ducks behind the wagon.

Hawk, kneeling beside the wagon, FIRES again.

Another Pawnee is hit; pitches off his horse.

Hawk takes a closer look at the attacking group and sees:

The Pawnee are being led by Red Knife, on horseback. Red Knife spots Hawk; recognizes him. The adversaries' eyes momentarily lock, then Red Knife is lost behind one of his attacking braves.

Andrews recovers from his fall, grabs his Henry and crawls under the wagon. He turns to Hawk.

      ANDREWS
  Thought all Indians were "brothers"?

      HAWK
   (A silent "Humph!")
  Not Pawnee.
He FIRES again at the attacking Pawnee.

From behind the wagon, Running Wolf FIRES his rifle at the approaching Pawnee. He misses. Crow Woman hands him an extra rifle from the back of the wagon; reloads the one he has just fired.

In unison, Hawk and Andrews FIRE their Henrys at the attackers.

Two more Pawnee fall. The other attackers hesitate at the superior firepower, then, led by Red Knife, withdraw.

                    ANDREWS
                 (As he reloads)
              Love the Henry.

A bullet, fired from a different direction, slams into the base of the wagon, just missing Andrews.

                    ANDREWS
                    (Startled)
            Jesus!

He turns and sees:

From behind a large rock about a hundred yards away, two other Pawnee FIRE at the wagon.

                    ANDREWS
                   (Continuing)
              They got us in a crossfire.

Hawk and Andrews move back under the wagon. Hawk FIRES toward the rock.

                    HAWK
            This no good. We too much in open.
                    ANDREWS
                 (Indicates their
                    Henrys)
              These'll keep 'em away.

                    HAWK
            Come dark, they not help us see.

Both men survey the terrain in front of them. There are no Pawnees in sight. CONTINUING SOUND of the infant crying.

                    HAWK
                    (Calls)
              Mrs. Carver, are you all right?

INT. SCHOONER WAGON. AFTERNOON.

Rebecca, clutching the baby to her, lies low behind the boxes.

                    REBECCA
         (Calls)
        Just scared.

EXT. THE PRAIRIE. AFTERNOON.

Hawk and Andrews crouch low under the wagon.

                    ANDREWS
       Got any ideas, Indian?

                      HAWK
       One, white man.

Staying low, he crawls toward the rear of the wagon; motions to Running Wolf. The youth kneels next to him.

                      HAWK
        (To Running Wolf)
       Take pony. Ride to valley of
       the tall grass.

Running Wolf nods; crouches low, as he makes his way to his horse.

Hawk turns to Crow Woman.

                      HAWK
        (Continuing)
      "Keep low, my mother."

Crow Woman crouches beneath the wagon. Running Wolf leaps onto his horse.

HAWK
              (Shouts to Andrews)
          Cover him!

Hawk and Andrews begin FIRING their rifles toward the large rock, as Running Wolf bolts his horse in the opposite direction. There is no return fire.

Running Wolf disappears into the distance, and the men cease firing.

                    ANDREWS
          Now what?

                    HAWK
          We wait for him to come back.
              (Beat)
          You know Oregon country?

                    ANDREWS
          My folks got a ranch near the Snake
          River.

                    HAWK
          You pretty young to lead wagons.

                    ANDREWS
          You're pretty young to be a
          warrior chief.

Hawk resists a smile.

                    HAWK
          You fight in white man's war?

                    ANDREWS
              (Nods; slaps his leg)
          Caught a ball in my leg at
          Chickamauga.

                    HAWK
              (Beat)
       Thought all white men "brothers."

Andrews resists a smile.

                              DISSOLVE TO:

EXT. THE PRAIRIE. NIGHT.

The night is dark... quiet. The schooner wagon sits alone on the plain. Its occupants waiting... watching...chewing on Rebecca's pre-baked biscuits. Andrews is still under the wagon; Gruber remains behind a wheel on the opposite side.

                   ANDREWS
         You see anything, Mr. Gruber?

                    GRUBER
              (Shakes head; German
              accent)
         Nein.... Worried about wife...
         children.

INT. SCHOONER WAGON. NIGHT.

Rebecca rocks the baby; chews on a biscuit. Hawk crawls into the wagon from the rear.

                    HAWK
         Mrs. Carver....

                   REBECCA
              (Formal)
         Mr. Hawk.

                    HAWK
       You should not worry. Running Wolf
       will be back soon with my brothers.

                    REBECCA
You sure they'll come?

                    HAWK
Even Crazy Buffalo hates Pawnee more
than he hates me.
          (Beat)
Thank you... for what you said to Andrews.

                    REBECCA
I was just tellin' the truth.

                    HAWK
I talk to him. He will take you to
Oregon with the other wagons.
                    REBECCA
          (Beat)
Guess that's all right.

                    HAWK
He good man. Remind me a little of
Mr. Carver.

                    REBECCA
He's dead.

                    HAWK
          (Beat)
You keep horses... food.... Trade
what you not need.

He turns to exit the wagon.

                    REBECCA
Mr. Hawk....

                    HAWK
Yes, Mrs. Carver?

                    REBECCA
            You gotta tell me somethin'.

                    HAWK
    Yes?

                    REBECCA
                (Beat)
            You <u>said</u> you had feelin's for me.

He studies her for a long moment.

                    HAWK
            Mrs. Carver... I have looked into
            my heart.... I <u>have</u> feelings for
            you.... They are deep.
                (Beat)
            Mrs. Carver should now look into <u>her</u>
            heart.
                (Beat)
            She must know that these times are not
            good.... Does she want the struggle that
            will come between our peoples to make
            enemies of us?

Rebecca begins to accept the truth of their situation, as they stare at each other for a long moment.

                                        CUT TO:

EXT. THE PRAIRIE. NIGHT.

From under the wagon, Andrews spots something in the distance.

                    ANDREWS
                (To himself)
            Oh, Jesus!

INT. SCHOONER WAGON. NIGHT.

Rebecca and Hawk are as we last saw them.

                    ANDREWS (O.S.)
          (Continuing)
    Hey, Indian!

The moment broken, Hawk quickly exits the wagon through the rear.

EXT. THE PRAIRIE. NIGHT.

A horrified Andrews and Gruber stand next to each other looking off into the distance, as Hawk emerges from the wagon. He joins them, follows their gaze and sees:

The horizon is red; aglow with fire.

                    ANDREWS (O.S.)
    They've set fire to the wagon train!

Gruber panics; rushes to his horse, muttering:

                    GRUBER
    My wife! My children!

He mounts; gallops off toward the horizon. Andrews walks over; grabs the reins of Jacob's horse.

                    ANDREWS
          (To Hawk)
    We could use you and yer Henry.

                    HAWK
          (Hesitant)
    Must stay here. Protect Mrs. Carver.

                    ANDREWS
          (As he mounts; angry)
     They ain't attackin' this wagon!
     They're after ones with women and
     children in 'em.
          (Harsh)
     Or, do you Indians only kill "brothers"
     to save yer own skin?

He gives his horse a kick; gallops off after Gruber. Hawk watches him disappear into the darkness. He'd like to go with him, but he's torn. He moves back toward the rear of the wagon.

Rebecca sticks her head out of the wagon.

                    REBECCA
     What's happened!?!

                    HAWK
     Pawnee set fire to wagon train.

                    REBECCA
     Why don't you go help 'em?

                    HAWK
     I stay with you.

                    REBECCA
     They need you more than I do, right
     now.... You said Running Wolf'll be
     back soon....
          (Produces a Colt from
          behind a box)
     We got guns.... Crow Woman and me'll
     be all right 'til he gets here.

Hawk thinks a moment, then turns to Crow Woman, who has been crouched under the wagon.

                          HAWK
               "Stay close to her, my mother."

Crow Woman nods. Hawk, momentarily, turns back to Rebecca, a feeling of true affection radiating from his eyes. Then, he mounts one of the horses; gallops off after Andrews.

The two women watch him disappear into the night, then look at each other.

                                        CUT TO:

EXT. ANOTHER PART OF THE PRAIRIE. NIGHT.

CAMERA TRACKS Andrews and Gruber galloping toward the glowing horizon. Suddenly, they rein their horses, hearing the SOUND of a horse approaching from behind at a faster gallop. Rifles ready, they turn and see:

Hawk appears out of the darkness; rides over to them.

Andrews gives the Cheyenne a quick nod of appreciation, and, with CAMERA TRACKING, the three men continue toward the horizon.

After a few moments, Hawk reins his horse; listens. Andrews and Gruber also hesitate. Hawk dismounts; studies the ground.

                          GRUBER
                         (Angry)
                    We must hurry!

                          HAWK
                         (Beat)
                    This not right.

He remounts.

>   HAWK
>   (Continuing)
>   Pawnee double back.

He turns his horse; rides back in the direction from which he came.

>   ANDREWS
>   (Confused)
>   What the hell!?!
>   (Beat; angry)
>   Damn Indians!!

He and Gruber head their horses toward the glowing horizon.

>   CUT TO:

EXT. THE PRAIRIE. NIGHT.

The schooner wagon is as we last saw it. Crow Woman sits against the rear wheel, holding a front loading musket to her chest.

Rebecca is on the front seat of the wagon; holding the Colt. She listens intently to the NIGHT SOUNDS. Behind her, inside the wagon, we see the baby asleep in a makeshift cradle.

A SNAP; perhaps a twig. Crow Woman stands, and holding her weapon ready, listens intently. She moves a few steps away from the wagon.

Unaware of Crow Woman's movements, Rebecca continues to listen. Suddenly, she hears a LOW GURGLE behind her. She turns; listens closely. Nothing. And, there is no movement behind her.

Rebecca, again, turns front. She is startled to see:

Using the oxen as cover, a Pawnee Warrior is creeping up on her.

Rebecca gasps.

Realizing that he has been spotted, the Indian stops for a brief moment; leers at her. Then, he makes a leap at her.

Rebecca produces the Colt; FIRES at her attacker.

The Pawnee is hit; falls dead on to the ground.

Screaming a chilling war cry, Another Pawnee Warrior rushes her from the other side of the oxen.

Rebecca FIRES TWICE at him.

The Indian staggers; falls.

INT. SCHOONER WAGON. NIGHT.

Behind Rebecca, the baby starts to CRY. Rebecca spins and sees:

Red Knife is inside the wagon. A vengeful, sadistic grin is on his face. In one hand he holds a Bowie knife. In his other arm, he has Rebecca's baby.

>   REBECCA
>   (Frightened)
>   Hawk <u>said</u> you'd be back.

Slowly, agonizingly, Red Knife brings the knife over toward the shrieking infant's throat.

>   REBECCA
>   (Screams)
>   <u>No</u>!

Rebecca thinks fast. She drops the Colt; rips open the front of her dress, exposing her breasts.

Red Knife hesitates; ogles her. He puts the baby back into the cradle, then, keeping his knife out, moves toward Rebecca.

Rebecca turns her head in disgust, as the aroused Indian reaches out to touch her breast.

A SHOT hits Red Knife square in the forehead. A stunned expression on his face, he falls backwards into the wagon.

Rebecca spins around and sees:

Standing next to the oxen, Hawk lowers the smoking Henry.

As Rebecca covers herself and grabs the crying child, Hawk moves up closer to the wagon.

> REBECCA
> (Rocking baby)
> Oh... baby... baby....

> HAWK
> Setting fire to wagons was trick to draw us away from here.

EXT. THE PRAIRIE. NIGHT.

Hawk assists Rebecca, as she climbs down from the front seat, holding the baby.

> REBECCA
> How many times you gonna save my life?

> HAWK
> You save me, too.

Rebecca impulsively embraces Hawk with her free arm. He is, initially, uncomfortable, then he slowly, tentatively, puts his arms around her. They stand like that for a moment, until he sees:

Crow Woman lies face down a few feet from the rear of the wagon.

Hawk leaves Rebecca; rushes over to kneel next to his mother. Her throat has been cut.

      REBECCA (O.S.)
    (Weeping)
 Oh, no!

There are tears behind Hawk's eyes, but they will not come. Rebecca moves up behind Hawk; puts her hand on his shoulder.

      REBECCA
 I'm so sorry.

Hawk begins to sing the Cheyenne funeral chant. Still weeping, Rebecca moves back to give him some privacy.

SOUND of horses approaching.

Running Wolf, followed by Tall Elk, Crazy Buffalo, Yellow Moccasin and the other Cheyenne ride up to the wagon; rein their horses. Seeing Crow Woman's body, they react with sorrow.

      TALL ELK
    (To Hawk, still on his
    knees)
 "We grieve with you, my brother."

Hawk rises; grasps the Henry.

      HAWK
    (With determination)
 "We will help the whites. The
 Pawnee who did this are attacking
 their wagon train."

The Cheyenne, including Crazy Buffalo, nod in agreement. Hawk mounts his horse; turns to Running Wolf and Yellow Moccasin.

> HAWK
> (Continuing)
> "Yellow Moccasin and Running Wolf
> will stay and protect Mrs. Carver."

The others nod, as Yellow Moccasin and Running Wolf dismount.

Hawk looks at Rebecca with affection. The look is returned.

> HAWK
> (Continuing; to Rebecca)
> You will be safe.

Then, he rides off in the direction of the wagon train. The other Cheyenne follow. Rebecca watches them disappear; turns and smiles at Running Wolf. It is a sad smile.

> SLOW DISSOLVE TO:

EXT. ANOTHER PART OF THE PRAIRIE. DAY.

An open plain, near a ravine. On a hill above, the Cheyenne warriors, including Tall Elk, Crazy Buffalo, Yellow Moccasin, Running Wolf and the others, observe the wagon train, consisting of eleven wagons, getting ready to depart to continue the journey west.

The Pioneer Men, Women and Children load the last of their belongings into the wagons. The canvas coverings of some have been burned away, but, in general, the damage is slight.

Not far from the wagons are four freshly dug graves with Crosses atop them.

Near the lead wagon, Andrews, on horseback, confers with Gruber, Gruber's lanky blond son, PETER, 18, and two other men. Rebecca stands next to her wagon, talking to Hawk who holds the reins of his horse in one hand and the Henry in his other. Eyeing Hawk with mistrust and apprehension from nearby, and doing a poor job of not being obvious about it, are several Pioneer Women and Children.

> HAWK
> (To Rebecca;
> indicating Henry)
> Thank you, Mrs. Carver.

> REBECCA
> You use it a lot better than I do.
> (Beat)
> You take care yerself. Remember you're the cautious mountain lion. Don't go after the grizzly bear.

> HAWK
> (Smiles)
> I will remember.
> (Beat)
> I will miss you, Mrs. Carver.

Off to one side, the Pioneer Women continue to watch the couple; whisper among themselves in German.

> REBECCA
> I'll miss you, Mr. Hawk.
> (Beat)
> Maybe you'll come to Oregon for a visit some day?

> HAWK
> I will try.

She knows that he won't, as she abruptly holds out her hand.

                    REBECCA
          Goodbye.

He takes her hand; shakes it.

                    HAWK
          Goodbye, Mrs. Carver.

He mounts his horse; looks over at the Pioneer Women, who return his gaze with paranoid stares. Suddenly:

                    HAWK
              (Barks loudly at Women)
          Ruff!!

The Women shriek; scurry off with their children.

Hawk and Rebecca's eyes meet, and they share a laugh. Then, Hawk kicks his horse; gallops toward the hill to join the other Cheyenne.

Rebecca, holding back tears, watches him ride off until she hears her baby CRYING from inside the wagon. As she climbs onto the front seat, Andrews rides up, followed by Peter, who is on foot.

                    ANDREWS
          Ma'm, this here is Mr. Gruber's
          son, Peter. He's offered to
          drive yer wagon for ya.

                    REBECCA
          Thank you.

Rebecca retrieves the infant from the back of the wagon, as Peter climbs up onto the front seat; takes the reins.

EXT. HILLTOP. DAY.

Hawk joins his fellow Cheyenne; turns and looks back at the departing wagons. There is sadness in his eyes.

EXT. THE PRAIRIE. DAY.

The wagons start to move.

CAMERA TRACKS Rebecca's wagon. She sits on the front seat, holding the baby, as Peter drives the oxen.

> PETER
> (German accent)
> A pretty baby, Frau Carver.
> What is his name?

> REBECCA
> Matthew.
> (Beat)
> Matthew Hawk Carver.

She glances back over her shoulder and sees:

Hawk and the Cheyenne watching from the hilltop.

She smiles to herself; looks forward.

OVERHEAD SHOT

The Cheyenne continue to watch the wagon train as it moves off toward the Rocky Mountains, looming in the distance.

THE END

158 * CHEYENNE WARRIOR

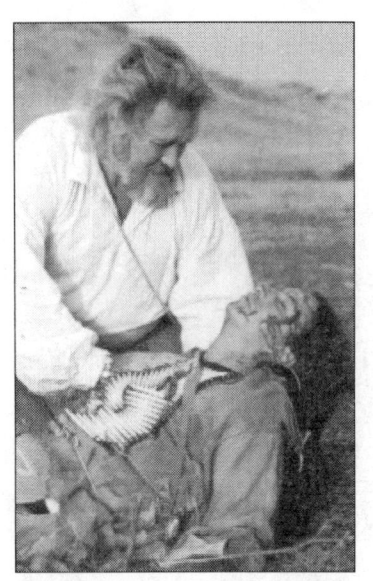

Dan Haggerty and Pato Hoffmann

Kelly Preston and Rick Dean

Kelly Preston and Pato Hoffmann

Kelly Preston and Dan Clark

Kelly Preston and Pato Hoffmann

Kelly Preston

Pato Hoffmann and Bob Hopkins

Dan Haggerty

Pato Hoffmann

Patricia Van Ingen

Kelly Preston

CHEYENNE WARRIOR

Afterword

AFTERWORD

Reminisces of **Cheyenne Warrior**
[*From the writer's viewpoint*]

The Script

"Good script," my agent said, "but I don't know where I'd send it."

"What are you talking about?" I retorted. "Westerns are popular again. Everybody's making them."

"Yeah, but this is too soft. It's not really a western. It's a love story."

"So, what's wrong with a love story?"

I forget his answer, but that pretty much ended that conversation.

Over the next year or two, my agent sent **The Cheyenne Warrior** out a few times, but, basically, it remained on his shelf. Even the success of Clint Eastwood's **Unforgiven** (1992) didn't motivate him to push my script.

January, 1993: I was still running my own public relations business, as I had been since the mid-1960s, when, one day, I received a call from Lance Robbins, then Vice-President in charge of Development at Saban Entertainment. He was interested in hiring a personal publicist. At his invitation, I went to his office and pitched him.

I didn't get the p.r. account, but while I was in Lance's office, the discussion turned to screenplays. He invited me to submit him something. I sent over **The Cheyenne Warrior**.

That's the last I heard from him, until:

August, 1993: The publicity business was lousy. I, in fact, was in the process of buying another type of (non-entertainment oriented) business altogether, when, out of the blue, Lance phoned me.

"Is **The Cheyenne Warrior** still available?" he asked.

I assured him that it was.

"I like this script," he said. "We want to do it."

The "we" was actually a co-production between Saban, which would distribute the film to markets outside the United States, and producer/director Roger Corman's company, Concorde/New Horizons, which would actually make the movie and handle domestic distribution.

Within two days of that phone call, my agent had negotiated a satisfactory deal for my screenplay, and Cheyenne Warrior was scheduled to begin filming the following month.

Production

"Where are you going to shoot this?" I asked the line producer, Mike Elliott, in one of our early (soon to be frequent) phone conversations. "It's set, you know, on the Great Plains."

"We'll be filming just outside of Los Angeles."

"Where!?!" I attempted to stay calm while picturing my story being re-set in the Mojave Desert.

"Don't worry," Michael assured me. "We've found this great ranch out in the Simi Valley [located Northwest of Los Angeles]. It's just off the freeway, about a mile from the Ronald Reagan Library. If we point the camera in the right direction, you'll never know that we're not east of the Rockies.

I must admit that he was absolutely right.

The ranch on which the shell of the trading post was built and almost all of the exterior scenes were shot was, indeed, located just behind an upper middle class housing tract and golf course, but when that film footage was intercut with second-unit material photographed against some snow-capped California mountains, the actors were, indeed, on the "Great Plains."

I'm told that, when the folks at Saban first viewed the final film, their initial comment was: "We didn't know that you went to Canada to shoot this."

I visited the location on several occasions, including the first day of filming. The first scene to be shot that day was the one in which Kearney and Nielsen kill Matthew Carver. Interestingly, director Mark Griffiths staged that scene only a few feet in back of the trading post facade, yet, in the story, the incident takes place miles away. Indeed, at no time during the four week exterior shooting schedule did the company venture more than a few hundred yards from that spot.

And, while Griffiths worked with his first team of actors, the second unit, led by co-producer Alba Francesca, toiled constantly. For example, except for the close shots in which the key actors are recognizable, the entire action sequence in which Hawk and his two companions attack Kearney and Nielsen's wagon was staged with doubles.

Ms. Francesca is quite a creative movie-maker who knows when to take advantage of an opportunity.

During the final week of filming, the catastrophic Malibu fire was raging some miles away from the ranch location. Late in the day, the blaze crested a hill in the distance, and Alba turned her camera toward it.

That shot near the end of the picture of the wagon train burning in the distance is actually the Malibu fire.

On the other hand, there were times when no amount of ingenuity could solve the lack-of-money problem.

You'll note that much of <u>Cheyenne Warrior</u> takes place during the dead of winter...yet there is no snow on the ground. "Fake snow is too expensive," producer Elliott replied to my questioning the absence of this important set dressing. "We can't afford it."

"How are you going to suggest winter?" I persisted.

"We'll dress the actors in heavy clothing. The audience won't know the difference."

And, you know, he was right. I don't think that the missing snow bothered anybody but me.

Lack of money was also the reason why Andrews' (Bo Hopkins) wagon train at the end of the film consisted of only three wagons. Perhaps we should have re-named it a wagon *shuttle*.

Cheyenne Warrior may have been filmed on a *minimum* budget, but with inventive planning and on-the-spot creativity, it certainly had the look of a five-million-dollar picture. Roger Corman and his people are very good at that.

Casting

For one brief moment, it looked like John Travolta might play Matthew Carver, Rebecca's short-lived husband, in the film. Travolta, as his fans are well aware, is married to Kelly Preston, who had been cast in the leading role. The couple thought it might be fun to work together.

This occurred shortly *before* Pulp Fiction (the film that catapulted Travolta back into super stardom status) was released, thus Mike Elliott thought that he might, indeed, be able to snag the actor for that role.

"His manager demanded an outrageous fee for one day's work," recalls the producer, "plus a percentage deal.

"On our budget, that was totally out of the question...even if Travolta worked a week, which is how long it would take to complete his part."[*]

Charles Powell played Matthew Carver.

---

[*] In filmmaking, acting deals are based, in part, on how many days (or weeks) a performer will be needed to complete his particular role. Whenever possible, a wise producer will schedule secondary parts so that their scenes are bunched together and can be shot quickly; hopefully in a matter of days. This common practice allows for the casting of an otherwise financially unattainable actor to be utilized in a key part. For example, in the movie Dillinger and Capone (1995), based on my original screenplay, the producers were able to hire Academy Award winner F. Murray Abraham to play Al Capone because the shooting schedule was set up so that his entire co-starring role could be shot in five (5) days.

Many talented young actresses were up for the part of Rebecca Carver, but aside from Kelly Preston (<u>Mischief</u>, <u>Twins</u>), the only one who was given serious consideration was Ione Skye (<u>River's Edge</u>, <u>Say Anything</u>).

At the time <u>Cheyenne Warrior</u> was made, Ms. Skye might have possessed a slightly better known name, but with Preston's subsequent roles in movies like <u>Citizen Ruth, Addicted to Love</u> and <u>Jerry Maguire</u>, that certainly has changed to our film's benefit.

I was delightfully surprised when I'd learned that we'd snagged Bo Hopkins for the role of Andrews, the wagon master. He's an actor I'd always admired and, I was informed that he'd decided to accept this relatively short role because he wasn't busy and, as he said, "I've never played a wagon master."

We wanted a "name" for the part of Barkley, operator of the trading post. I'd always envisioned the character as a crotchety, lovable "Walter Brennan" type. Wilford Brimley, had he a bigger name, would've been ideal.

Robert Duvall was the first actor approached by the producer. I hoped that I was wrong, yet I *knew* that there was no way that he would do it. Even though it would take less than a week to film that role in its entirety, his asking price was totally out of reach of the movie's budget.

Other actors considered for the part who either proved too expensive or unavailable were Richard Widmark, Charlton Heston, Jack Palance, and even George Peppard, with whom, at one point, Mike Elliott thought we might make a deal.

I even recall suggesting Dennis Weaver, but Elliott said "No!"

Indeed, the casting of Barkley became a real cliffhanger.

Dan Haggerty ("Grizzly Adams") was hired to play the role two days before it was to begin shooting.

Dan is a very nice man and, I think, that his performance was effective. I just wish that he'd brought a bit more humor to the role. Certainly that aspect of the character was strongly infused in my script.

"You s.o.b.," Dan said to me with a grin when we first met on the set. "This is the first time I've ever been killed in a movie!"

The biggest casting challenge was the native American roles.

At one time, my good friend Michael Ansara, who has played dozens of Indians on screen, from Cochise in the old "Broken Arrow" television series to the "Centennial" mini-series, would have played a key role in <u>Cheyenne Warrior</u>. He was Hollywood's favorite Indian...even though he is of Lebanese descent.

Today, however, in our world of "political correctness," Native Americans are played by Native Americans.

Does that also mean that only a Lebanese can play a Lebanese?

The problem is that there is a vast shortage of Native American actors, who are "names." Graham Greene (<u>Dances With Wolves</u>, <u>Thunderheart</u>) and Wes Studi (<u>The Last of the Mohicans</u>, <u>Geronimo: An American Legend</u>) are definite exceptions, but they're *character* actors. The role of Hawk called for a *leading man*.

"We made an offer to Rodney A. Grant (<u>Dances With Wolves</u>, <u>Son of the Morning Star</u>), but he was asking more than we could afford to pay," recalls Mike Elliott. "We decided that we would cast an unknown."

Pato Hoffmann, who'd previously filmed a small, but showy role in <u>Geronimo: An American Legend</u>, was cast as Hawk, his first leading role in a movie. Pato is Aymara/Quechua (Inca).

Runner-up for that plumb was Dan Clark, a Cherokee, who was awarded the part of Red Knife, leader of the villainous band of Pawnees, and Patricia Van Ingen, also Cherokee, a former dancer in such films as <u>Kismet</u> (1955), played Hawk's mother, Crow Woman.

Interestingly, filling the Pawnee roles was not an easy task. Several of Hollywood's Native American actors actually refused to play members of a tribe that, according to history, had severely brutalized other peoples.

Co-producer Alba Francesca told me that many of the young men who were interviewed for roles were very aware of their cultural roots. "Asking them to play a Pawnee," she said, "would be like offering the part of a Nazi to a Jewish actor."

There was one final piece of casting yet to be done in <u>Cheyenne Warrior</u>. That was the role of Gruber, Andrews' companion, who in a revised version of my script, gets shot in the back with an arrow before he gets to utter a word.

I decided that that part should be mine. After all, if Alfred Hitchcock could make an appearance in *his* films....

"Sorry," Mike Elliott said, "the role is taken."

I saw my chance for a stellar acting career disappearing fast. "Who's playing it?" I asked.

"Me!"

Producers! Humph!

The Finished Film

I don't recall the date, but the first time I saw Cheyenne Warrior put together was in its rough cut form. The occasion was a private screening for people who'd worked on the film. There was no music, titles or optical effects, yet I knew that we had a winner. The movie worked, and even though minor changes and adjustments had been made on my original script, I felt that the producers had remained true to my work.

I did, however, have a couple of editing suggestions for director Mark Griffiths. "The shootings have to be tighter," I told him. "Right now, it looks like the Indians are standing there, waiting to be shot."

That was an easy change. All that was needed was for the editor to remove one or two frames from the shots of both the "shooter" and the "shootee."

My other suggestion was a little more difficult to accomplish.

In telescoping my original screenplay, the producer and director had inserted the "banquet" scene with Rebecca, Hawk and his Cheyenne brothers, which takes place outside of the trading post. They had made that a Christmas scene, in which Rebecca tells the Indians about the Christ child and so forth.

"That *can't* be a Christmas scene," I said to Mark. "There is *no way* that they would be dining outside on the Great Plains in the middle of winter."

He saw my point, and you'll note that, in the film, there is no reference to Christmas in that sequence.

The final version of Cheyenne Warrior runs 86-minutes. The rough cut that I saw was several minutes longer than that. Removed in the interim were the night scene with Rebecca and Matthew in their wagon *after* they meet Hawk in the trading post, plus Rebecca's second graveside chat with Matthew.

According to a former employee at Concorde/New Horizons, "Roger Corman likes a snappy movie. No film could run over 90-minutes."

As I've said previously, I'm quite happy with the finished picture. The performances are exceptional, particularly those of Pato Hoffmann and Rick Dean, a Concorde "regular," who plays Kearney.

Of the three produced films that were based on one of my original scripts, it's the only one of which I'm truly proud. I love Arthur Kempel's musical score, particularly his main theme, and, I think that cinematographer Blake T. Evans' day-for-night scenes are among the very best I've ever seen. Indeed, I was surprised recently when Mike Elliott informed me that those sequences *were* day-for-night.

I thank everybody who contributed to the production.

Cheyenne Warrior was ready for release in the summer of 1994. For a time, there was serious talk about releasing it into theaters first, but, since Concorde/New Horizons needed a home video title to fill their summer slot, the movie was relegated to just one or two theaters (to satisfy Screen Actors Guild requirements). Then, in August, it appeared on the shelves in your local video store. A lengthy run on HBO/Cinemax followed.

Script Changes

Script changes on any film are inevitable. The *legitimate* reasons for changes are infinite. A line doesn't sound as good as it read on paper. A scene doesn't play. A sequence, as written, is too expensive to shoot.

In my original screenplay for <u>Dillinger and Capone</u>, for example, the final shoot-out was set on Al Capone's yacht. That was the first thing to be changed. Executive producer Roger Corman insisted that the scene be staged in Capone's mansion, because sequences shot on the water are *very* expensive to shoot.

If you doubt that, do a little research into the filming of <u>Jaws</u>, and you'll see why that classic thriller went way over its original budget.

Most of the changes in <u>Cheyenne Warrior</u> had to do with cutting an approximately 120-page script down to about 90-pages. Characterization and texture were forced to step aside in favor of a faster pace.

One scene that I *was* sorry to lose was the sequence in which Running Wolf, the young Indian lad, spies on Rebecca while she is bathing in the stream. It was an amusing moment, but, alas, it's my understanding that Kelly Preston nixed doing a nude scene.

Sometimes changes can create tensions. There *were* a couple of heated discussions:

At one point prior to the start of filming, producer Elliott was seriously considering altering the ending of the story. He wanted Hawk and Rebecca to wind up together.

"There is no way," I said, "considering the time that this story takes place, that they could stay together. It would ruin the picture."

I guess that Mike realized that I was right on that one. The ending *didn't* change.

[Hmmm! I wonder if that's the *real* reason why I didn't get to play Gruber.]

One dispute that I lost was with director Mark Griffiths. In my original script, the relationship between Rebecca and Hawk remains platonic through the end. In Griffith's version, however, this is not the case. Worse still, his suggested love-making scene occurs *before* my scene, in which Hawk says to Rebecca, "I have feelings for you."

If those scenes had been reversed, I *still* wouldn't've liked it, but it *might've* worked. As it now stands, I feel that Rebecca comes off as a bit of a slut...and that was *not* my intention.

Remember, in The King and I, from which the basic idea for this film sprang, Anna and the King never went to bed together.

For the record, Mike Elliott agrees with me on that point, but he was unable to change the director's mind either.

•••

Henry Hull has a delightful line in Jesse James (1939), the classic Tyrone Power/Henry Fonda western. He plays a cantankerous newspaper publisher, who is always writing an editorial that starts something like: "If the West is ever going to become civilized, we're going to have to take all the railroad presidents out and shoot them down like dogs."

Now, that's pretty much how I sometimes feel about directors...or producers...or actors...who try to change my scripts.

But, God bless 'em! We still need them.

CHEYENNE WARRIOR

Cast and Crew

Cast

Kelly Preston
    Rebecca Carver
Pato Hoffmann
    Hawk
Bo Hopkins
    Andrews
Rick Dean
    Kearney
Clint Howard
    Otto Nielsen
Charles Powell
    Matthew Carver
Dan Clark
    Red Knife
Winterhawk
    Tall Elk
Joseph Wolves Kill
    Running Wolf
Patricia Van Ingen
    Crow Woman
Dan Haggerty
    Barkley

•••

Behind the Scenes

Producer:
    Mike Elliott

Co-Producer:
    Alba Francesca

Exec. Producer:
    Roger Corman
    Lance H. Robbins

Assoc. Producer:
    Mike Upton

Director:
    Mark Griffiths

Writer:
    Michael B. Druxman

Cinematographer:
Blake T. Evans

Editor:
Roderick Davis

Music Composer:
Arthur Kempel

Production Design:
Aaron Osborne

Set Decorator:
Jeanne Lusignan

Casting:
Mark Sikes

Sound:
Christopher Taylor

Costume Design:
Tami Mor Wyman

•••

Released by:
Concorde - New Horizons Corp.

MPAA rating:
PG

Parental rating:
Acceptable for children

Running time:
86

AVAILABLE ON VIDEO FROM NEW HORIZONS HOME VIDEO

KELLY PRESTON   DAN HAGGERTY

CHEYENNE WARRIOR

CONTACT INFORMATION: New Horizon Video • 5855 D Live Oak Parkway
Norcross, GA 30093 • (800) 845-3323

©1997 Concorde-New Horizons Corp. All Rights Reserved. Printed in USA.

NEW HORIZONS HOME VIDEO